The Handbook of Fly Tying

The Handbook of
FLY TYING

Peter Gathercole

The Crowood Press

First published in 1989 by
The Crowood Press
Ramsbury, Marlborough,
Wiltshire SN8 2HE

British Library Cataloguing in Publication Data

Gathercole, Peter
  The handbook of fly tying.
  1. Fly fishing. Flies. Tying. Manuals
  I. Title
  688.7'912

  ISBN 1-85223-047-9

Photographs by Peter Gathercole
Line-drawings by Graham Gaches

Typeset by Chippendale Type, Otley, West Yorkshire
Printed and bound in Spain by Graficas Estella, S.A. (Navarra)

Contents

Acknowledgements

When I first began to understand exactly what I had taken on with this project, I realised that no matter how much of the work I felt was all my own I still owed an enormous debt. Fly tying is very much an evolutionary process and anyone who begins to learn the skill depends greatly on those who went before, masters of the vice who have shaped fly tying into the subtle blend of art and craft it is today.

By learning each technique we are taking a short cut, aided by the inventiveness of others, who all had to develop methods for themselves. This process continues even today – perhaps even more so: with the confines of tradition removed and with a vast wealth of new and exciting materials, contemporary tyers are more adventurous than at any other time.

So to all the fly-tying innovators, past and present, whose patterns and techniques sprinkle the pages of this book, my thanks.

More specifically, I would like to thank Graham Gaches for his splendid line-drawings which complement a number of the tying sequences. Also Alan Bramley, Managing Director of hook makers Partridge of Redditch, for his help over the years.

Finally, I would like to thank all those who have helped and encouraged me in both my fly tying and my fishing. I count myself fortunate to have made many friends both at home and throughout the world simply because of fly fishing. I would like to list them all, but I'm not going to. It is certain I would manage to miss someone out somewhere along the line, so it is better and certainly more fitting that I thank everyone equally. After all, they know who they are.

1 Getting Started

As with any craft requiring a certain dexterity, it is a good idea to start fly tying right at the beginning. Many newcomers try something far too complex right at the outset, with the result that they become quickly disillusioned. Some give up completely, with the excuse that 'Fly tying is just far too difficult'. It isn't. You wouldn't expect to get in a car and drive it perfectly before learning about changing gear, steering, and so on. So it is with fly tying. To get a proper grounding you start with the basics, becoming familiar with the simpler methods before experience allows you to explore all the intricacies.

Tools

The first step is to choose the right tools for the job. Though it is possible to tie flies with just your fingers and a pair of scissors, most experienced tyers find that a selection of tools helps them produce flies more easily and quickly. Top of the list is a vice. As with all tools, it pays to buy the best you can afford. This doesn't mean you have to spend £50 or so right away, simply that you don't go to the other extreme in order to save money in case you don't like it. If you buy a very cheap vice, the odds are it will fail to hold the hook securely, making the task of tying a fly all the more difficult, which you don't want when starting off.

There are many types of vice on the market but my preference is for a simple lever-action model, with hardened steel jaws for durability and an adjustable stem to vary the height. I particularly like a lever-action vice because it is easy to obtain just the right tension to hold even very large hooks securely, which is very difficult

with the screw-tightened models. Most vice manufacturers produce acceptable models, some of which are virtual copies of the original Thompson Model A.

Scissors come next and whilst it is possible to get away with one pair it is best to have two. One can be the 'donkey' pair, used for cutting wire and tinsel – in fact anything tough. The second pair can then be kept for more precise work such as fine trimming and cutting thread. For the former a good small pair with wide, straight blades is best as they produce an even first-time cut. For the second pair some recommend curved blades but to be honest I prefer straight ones. Most important is that the blades are fine, very sharp and of good quality. Some of the surgical types work superbly and are well worth the expense.

Choice of hackle pliers is much the same. You can get away with one pair but two can be a great help, particularly as I always seem to mislay one at a crucial moment. All I ask of hackle pliers is that the jaws meet evenly and are smooth enough not to cut the hackle. The jaws may be serrated or rubber-coated, it matters not. Pliers come in a variety of sizes but I tend to stick to the medium-size types which allow the index finger to be inserted into the loop. This way the finger can be wound round the hook shank in a single smooth movement, which ensures that the hackle is laid down quickly, evenly and at the correct tension.

After the lever-action vice, the one other product which has really improved the speed and efficiency of tying flies is the spigot bobbin holder. Basically it is a pair of sprung wire arms, which hold the bobbin, with a tube through which to feed the thread. The sprung arms keep enough tension on the bobbin to prevent it unwinding until hand pressure is applied. The advantages are that the weight of the bobbin holder keeps the thread taut even when released and, because the thread is used directly off the bobbin, wastage is kept to a minimum.

For the last of the basic tools I would list the dubbing needle. Though it is called a dubbing needle, it is used for applying varnish and selecting wing slips as well as picking out fibres of dubbing. You can buy them ready-made but at a pinch a large darning needle is quite adequate and cheaper.

The tools already mentioned I consider essential, but other products can help immensely too. One is simplicity itself, the material spring, an ordinary fine spring joined at the ends and looped over the collar of the vice. Being bent, the coils open and provide a superb holder for keeping materials out of the way before winding on. It is something I would never be without.

The same cannot be said for some other tools. Hackle guards, gauges, hair stackers and wing selectors fall into this category. To a lesser extent so do half-hitch and whip-finish tools. Others might not agree but I prefer to use as few tools as possible. With a little practice it is easier and far quicker to use fingers alone, and they are also more adaptable to a new or tricky method.

If you do feel you need any of these tools, the list below should help.

Hackle Guard This tool is designed to hold back and prevent hackle fibres being trapped whilst a whip finish is being completed. The light metal strip contains a number of different-size holes which are slipped over the eye of the hook.

Hackle Gauge The gauge helps decide which length of hackle to choose, depending on the size of hook. Of help to beginners, experience soon makes it unneccessary.

Hair Stacker A metal tube into which a bunch

of hair is placed tips first. By tapping gently, the fibres drop until all the tips are even. A good idea, though the same effect is achieved if the bunch is held in a ring made by first finger and thumb.

Wing Selectors Various models are available and the basic idea is that two wire prongs separate a predetermined width of wing slip from a main quill, usually duck or goose. If you are tying large numbers of flies of the same size, this tool can be quite handy as it eliminates the need to judge the width each time and makes sure that both sides of the paired wing are even.

Whip-Finish and Half-Hitch Tools Though I did at one time use a whip-finish tool I now prefer to use my fingers. The technique is identical either way but quicker with the fingers alone (see Chapter 2). As far as the half hitch is concerned, I simply don't use it. For finishing off a fly it is a poor substitute for the whip finish.

Other tools and appliances which are necessary but less frequently used include wing cutters, fur blenders, and the like. For close-imitation dry flies the various types of wing cutter can be very useful. As a professional fly dresser I found them great for producing lifelike wings for ephemerid, caddis and stone-fly patterns, though for my own use I prefer a less clinical type of wing. Wing cutters come in two forms. The first works like a pastry cutter whilst the second, being brass, works as a heat sink, with excess material being burned away by a flame. Both work well on a wide range of hackles, quills and various man-made sheets, including foam.

Fur blenders are a particular favourite of mine as they open up whole new avenues to explore, especially in the imitation of nymphs and winged aquatic insects. The simplest is a teasel brush, used for fluffing up angora wool. Its stiff wires will pick out and blend fibres of wool or other materials and it is perfect for producing small quantities of experimental mixes. For

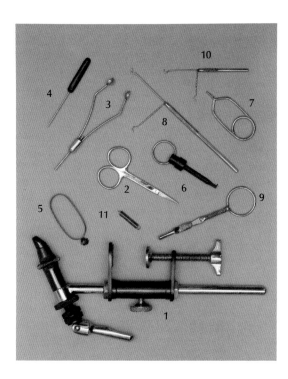

1. Lever-action vice with material spring in place round collar. 2. Scissors. 3. Spigot bobbin holder. 4. Dubbing needle.
5. Thompson's rubber-jaw hackle pliers.
6. Ezee hackle pliers. 7. Flat-jaw hackle pliers.
8. Whip-finish tool. 9. Sprung hackle pliers with serrated jaws. 10. Mini whip-finish tool.
11. Material spring – ends unjoined.

larger quantities a specialist electrical blender is ideal, though an ordinary food blender can be used. Blending is achieved with the addition of water and is very even and precise.

Hooks

A sound choice of hook is important for beginner and expert alike. Although there is a vast and bewildering array of hook shapes and sizes available it is not too difficult to sort out your requirements. Most suppliers of hooks produce a catalogue itemising and describing the patterns they stock.

As a general guide fly-tying hooks may be divided into four main groups. I use Partridge hooks, of high quality English manufacture, but a number of other makes are available. The models included below are personal favourites but other manufacturers' patterns may be substituted as required. The first category contains the standard wet-fly and nymph patterns. My preference is for a strong, medium-weight, round-bend model, favourite being the Partridge Captain Hamilton (L2A) and Captain Hamilton Nymph Hook (H1A). Both come in sizes ranging from a 4 to an 18, which is perfect for all but the tiniest midge or ephemerid tyings. For specialist pupae and bugs, particularly caddis, the Partridge K12ST fits the bill, with the K4A being ideal for shrimps and hoglice. For the very smallest patterns, the Vince Marinaro midge hook (K1A) is produced in sizes down to 28.

For dry flies I tend to stick to down-eyed hooks rather than the more traditional upturned eyes. Partridge's Captain Hamilton Standard Dry Fly (L3A) and Featherweight (L4A) hooks are my favourite barbed patterns, though I have been using the Roman Moser Arrowpoint barbless (CS20) with success.

The third category takes in the lure or streamer hooks. These are longshanked hooks, used for dressing large fry patterns and other lures worked on both lake and reservoir, as well as for migratory trout in rivers. Because this style of fishing often means horsing specimen trout out of snags, longshanks need to be tough. The normal pattern I use is Partridge's 4X Bucktail/Streamer (D4A), but the extra-strong loop-eyed SEB lure hook (CS2 BL) takes some beating. For 'fly in the salt', or light-coloured dressings, which are easily stained when bronzed hooks get wet, the JS Sea Streamer (CS 11), with its silvered finish, is ideal.

Fourth of the main groups are the hooks used for salmon and other migratory species. Usually finished in black, with an upturned loop eye for strength, they come in three main types. These are single, double or treble points, of which the singles are used most frequently. For standard dressings I particularly like the classically shaped Bartleet (CS10), and for low water conditions the incredibly lightweight and strong Wilson (01). In doubles I usually use the standard Partridge salmon double (P) and the Wilson Low Water double (02), along with the Esmond Drury treble, which is a very efficient hooker.

Of course, if you are only intending to dress flies for one specific type of fishing, this list may be reduced considerably, but once you are happy with your selection of hooks, materials are the next consideration.

Materials

It would be inappropriate to list all the materials available to the fly tyer; in any case many are actually mentioned during the tying sequences. Better to discuss the problems encountered regarding selection and storage.

Most of us obtain our materials from the various retail outlets, be they the local tackle shop or one of the big mail order catalogues. The vast majority of materials sold nowadays are of very high quality, most retailers being wary of their reputation. That said, quantities do vary so it pays to shop around. It also pays to buy the best, especially where hackles are concerned, the area with the greatest variation in quality. Beginners are often advised to buy cheap materials. In my experience this is not a good idea. Cheap, lower-quality materials are often more difficult to work with, particularly when it comes to hackles, which may be brittle or frayed. An added difficulty is the last thing anyone wants when trying to master a new skill.

Unfortunately there is a problem in obtaining top-quality hackles at the right price, particularly of the standard required for tying small dry flies. Some of the genetically-produced cock hackle and saddle capes available from the United States are of a superb quality. Henry Hoffman and Metz are two such brands, their top grade capes providing hackles small enough

to use on size 28 hooks as well as coming in all the right colours. They are expensive, though, at upwards of £50, but there is no waste and there are literally hundreds of usable feathers.

For most of us the Chinese and Indian capes provide the bulk of our hackles, though even these are getting scarce as demand outstrips supply. Again, careful shopping is the answer, along with getting to know a good, friendly supplier. Also, with the wonderfully effective floatants produced today it is possible to use slightly softer hackles than used to be the case. And in some instances, especially with large dries such as sedges, the extra 'suckability' of the soft hackle produces a more killing fly.

Apart from the retailer, other sources of materials include friends, local gamekeepers, and, of course, road casualties. Of all of these it is perhaps the gamekeeper who can be the most helpful, supplying anything from blue jay to pheasant and partridge, from grey squirrel tails to the occasional deer skin. Road kills such as fox, rabbit and badger can also come in handy but can be a mixed blessing. Most are too badly damaged to do anything with, or produce too much of one thing. However, any which are found in good condition can be popped into a large plastic bag ready for skinning and treating. Incidentally, has anyone found a use for hedgehog yet?

Once home, remove the skin, and scrape off as much of the fat and flesh as you can before pinning it to a board, hair or feather side down. If there is too much blood or dirt, wash thoroughly in warm, soapy water, drying off most of the water before pinning out. That done, rub the skin with a 1:1 mixture of alum and saltpetre, then leave it to cure slowly in a warm, dry place. Once it is completely dry, shake off the excess chemical and place the skin in a sealable poly-bag with a mothball or a similar product to prevent attack by creepy-crawlies.

It is a good idea to take this last precaution with all stored materials, even those which have been bought 'pest-free'. There is little worse than having expensive furs and feathers reduced to tatters by the larvae of the clothes moth. It usually occurs on those products which are being stored over a long period and the few pence it costs to prevent it are well spent.

Most fly dressers are inveterate hoarders and in only a few months find the collection they began with expanding out of all proportion. The answer is a decent storage system. This doesn't have to be complex or expensive so long as it keeps the materials in good condition, easily found and well separated from other similar products. If you haven't got one of the custom fly-tying cabinets, various pieces of office furniture can be pressed into service, and can be picked up quite cheaply second-hand. As long as they have plenty of drawer space and are easily moved they will be ideal. Because most materials are soft and easily compressible it is surprising just how much you can cram into a relatively small space.

Clear poly-bags, with sealable tops, are perfect for storing most fur and feathers. They come in a wide range of sizes and since they are clear, their contents are easily identified. If for any reason you receive anything too big to put in a bag – and I once was sent a whole whooper swan through the post – it may be broken down into its usable components for storage, the waste being discarded. For those who want to store large quantities of loose feathers, glass jars are a great alternative. Although they are much more bulky, they prevent delicate materials, such as barred wood duck, from being crushed and can make an attractive addition to your fly-tying den.

Smaller items such as dubbing materials and hooks can be kept either in small bags or in hard plastic containers. The clear plastic 'stack packs' are a very good idea. Hooks being stored in quantity should be left in their oiled paper wrappers for as long as possible; this will prevent them rusting. Once removed they can be placed in small plastic containers labelled with their size and type.

Tying threads and tinsels are a slightly different proposition. The greatest problem is preventing them from tangling together. For this reason it is best to keep them where they won't roll around. Also, remember before storing to catch the loose end in the notch cut into the spool by the manufacturer. Threads are best kept in dry conditions well away from direct sunlight, which can damage some of the finer sorts. Pure silk, for instance, can be badly weakened.

The Bench

Once tools, hooks and materials have been decided upon, you are ready to begin tying. One of the beauties of fly tying is that you don't need a great deal of money and space to become good – only practice. Any area where you can set up a small bench is quite adequate; you can even commandeer the kitchen table as a last resort.

If you do intend to set up a semi-permanent bench you will need to consider a few points. The first is the size of the working area. This needn't be large. Indeed, if I am any guide, the more space, the greater the mess! An area 24 inches square is fine, so long as it is at a comfortable height and will accept the table clamp of the vice. If a good table is being used it can be covered with a piece of light-coloured card, which not only protects against varnish spills but helps you see hooks and other small items. The thing to make sure of is that your work surface allows tools and materials to be spread in front of you so that they can be easily reached at every stage in the tying process.

Lighting is the next concern. A high-intensity lamp such as the Anglepoise is often recommended as a good source of illumination. Personally I don't like it, preferring a fluorescent tube where possible. I find that the more diffuse light given off by the strip is easier on the eyes, particularly when tying for long periods. Comfort is also enhanced by a properly-adjustable chair. Make sure that the one you use allows you to sit up straight. Arm rests are a definite advantage

Work bench.

too, as they give your elbows support during tricky or off-the-vice procedures. The right type of chair is very important. If you are not comfortable you will find it difficult to tie for long periods, you will tire quickly, and, worse, you could become prone to back problems in later years.

If you are setting up a semi-permanent bench, the type of flooring is worth a thought. Linoleum is ideal as any bits of waste material may be swept up and hooks easily found, which is not the case with carpeting. Either way it is a good idea to attach a small waste bag directly under the vice to catch all the bits. This can be bought or you can make it yourself by stretching a polythene bag over a wire coat-hanger bent

into a rectangular shape and fixed into position by trapping the wire between the table and the vice clamp. Cheap to produce, it saves a good deal of grief, especially if you are tying over the best carpet.

With this simple but comprehensive set-up, you are ready to begin tying. I have tried to be thorough, but if you feel that the selection of tools, hooks and materials is too much to begin with, take heart. When I began fly tying all I had was a simple pin vice attached to a wood clamp, and all my materials could be fitted into a small biscuit tin. Remember that in fly tying it is not the amount you spend on tools and materials which counts, but practice.

2 Preparatory Techniques

However aesthetically pleasing the outward appearance of a fly, it is all for nothing without sound preparatory technique. Flies are created to serve a practical purpose – to catch fish. The rigours of casting and fighting the fish soon put paid to delicate dressings and flies which haven't been tied properly. By this I don't mean how neatly the wing or hackle is tied on, but how the fly is constructed from the very first turn of thread. A strong, robust fly results from an equally strong base. Although it can't be seen once the pattern has been completed, poor technique reveals itself in a fly that quickly falls apart.

Sound technique begins right from putting the hook in the vice. An outwardly simple procedure, it is one that still causes problems. The usual advice is to use the jaws of the vice to mask the sharp hook point, to prevent the thread snagging. This works very well on medium to large flies, of standard tying, and is therefore good for the beginner; unfortunately, the jaws can block the area around the hook and hamper tying, particularly on very small hooks. Moreover, hooks with offset bends or special points, such as the Roman Moser Arrowpoint, can be easily damaged if pressure is put on the bend and point at the same time.

More important than masking the hook point is making sure that the hook is gripped firmly (you will find anyway that with practice you can easily avoid catching the thread on an exposed hook point). If the hook is forever moving around in the jaws it is difficult to get the correct thread tension and therefore difficult to tie the materials in properly. Achieving the correct pressure is easiest with the lever-type vice. You simply adjust the jaws until the gap is slightly greater than that of the hook wire, insert the hook to the required position, then depress the lever steadily. When gripped correctly there should be no vertical movement of the hook. A quick twang of the hook should produce a clear 'ping', indicating that it has been gripped firmly and is of the correct temper. Incidentally, although it is always a good idea to check a batch of hooks before tying, apart from the occasional misshape the quality of hooks sold is so good that you are unlikely to encounter any badly-tempered ones.

The Foundation

The type of tying thread to use is the next consideration. Pure silk is the traditional material, but today most use the modern nylons, which are stronger for a smaller diameter. They come in a range of strengths, the finest for tiny nymphs and dry flies, the strongest for large hairwings and Muddlers. Nylon thread also has the property of spreading itself flat when being wound, which makes it superb for keeping bulk to a minimum, particularly in smaller patterns. Silk, because it is a natural material, should be waxed before use. This has a twofold effect: it prevents the silk rotting and it helps the thread grip materials, which results in a more durable fly. Nylon thread won't rot in normal circumstances but it is still a good idea to wax it (or buy it pre-waxed) for the sake of durability.

Waxing the thread is a simple procedure. Just pull it through a lump of beeswax in a single smooth action, repeating it if necessary until the thread is properly coated. The friction caused by the smooth, quick draw actually melts the wax, which then adheres to the thread. Take care to make the action even as stopping will allow the wax to solidify and possibly break the thread.

The next step is to attach the tying thread to the hook. For a standard nymph, wet fly or streamer, the thread is caught in at the eye and then wound down the shank towards the bend. Although extremely easy once you know how, the technique can cause a few problems for the absolute beginner. Basically, one end of the tying thread (the waste end) is held in position whilst the other (the end that binds the fly together) is wound over it. This locks the thread on to the hook shank and allows further tight turns of thread to be made without them slipping off the shank and unravelling.

As an aid to clarity I have used red floss rather than normal tying thread to illustrate the techniques in this chapter: it is easier to see. The techniques may also be practised with floss until proficiency is achieved.

Attaching the Thread

Step 1

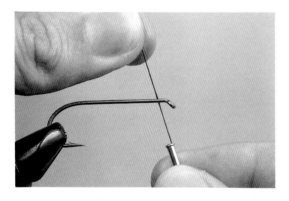

Fix the hook securely in the vice. Take hold of both ends of the thread and hold it against the far side of the hook shank.

Step 2

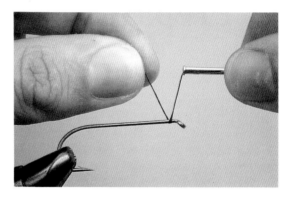

With the right hand take the thread under the shank, then up above it to form a V shape.

Step 3

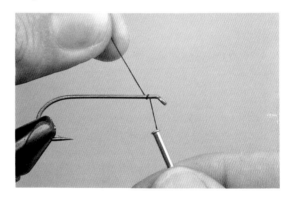

Keeping firm tension on the thread, simply begin to wind the bobbin-holder end down the hook shank in touching turns.

Step 4

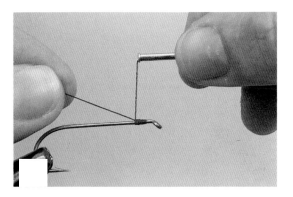

Continue winding for five or six turns, binding the loose end of thread down to the hook shank. This should be enough to prevent the thread from slipping. If the thread does still pull as you increase tension just make more turns until this stops.

Step 5

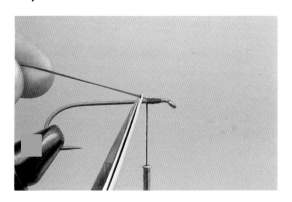

When the thread is firmly locked, trim off the waste end.

This foundation of thread – so often neglected – is essential in producing a durable fly. As you wind the thread along the hook shank make sure that the turns are tight and touching. This will provide a solid base on which the rest of the materials can grip. It will also provide an even foundation on which to wind tinsel bodies, preventing unsightly lumps and bumps forming.

Without it the dressing can actually revolve on the hook shank; at best this means that body or wing will fall out of alignment, at worst it will break the tension on the materials and allow them to come apart. Either way you end up with a fly which is useless.

Finishing Off

Including methods of finishing off the fly in a chapter on preparatory techniques isn't quite as crazy as it seems at first, for it is no good being able to tie a fly if you don't already know how to finish it off securely.

The Half Hitch

The simplest knot is the half hitch. It may be used either for finishing off a fly or keeping materials in place when the thread must be released. Although quick and easy, it is not a method I use often. Instead I allow the weight of the bobbin holder to keep tension on the thread. That stated, it is still a useful technique to know. If you don't use a bobbin holder it will come in handy for preventing the thread from unravelling between tying steps and will also help if the thread breaks accidentally. It *can* be used as a finishing knot, though I stress the word 'can' because, quite honestly, it is not man enough for the job, even when used in multiples.

Step 1

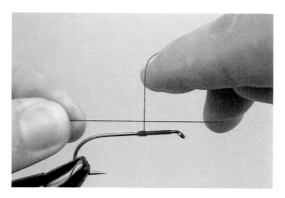

The half hitch may be used at any stage of the tying but here it is tied half-way down the hook shank. Keeping the thread taut with the left hand, with the forefinger and middle finger of the right hand pick up a loop in it, above the hook shank, in the form of a reversed figure 4.

Step 2

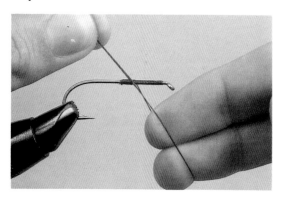

Twist the fingers round under the shank, throwing a single loop of thread over the hook eye.

Step 3

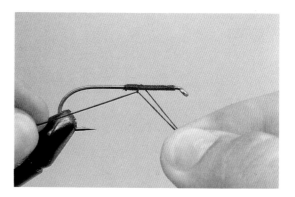

Using the thumb and forefinger of the right hand to keep tension, draw the loop closed with the left.

Step 4

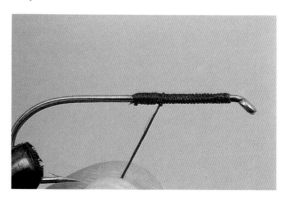

The half hitch.

By far the best way of putting the finishing touch to your well-tied fly is with a solid five-turn whip finish. This may be achieved either with your fingers or with the aid of a special whip-finish tool. Either will produce the required result though I prefer the former, finding it quicker. Still, there are those who will find it easier to use a tool and the picture sequences illustrate both methods.

The Hand Whip Finish

Step 1

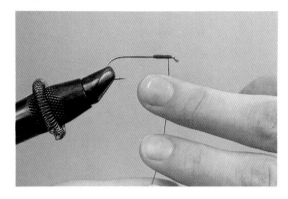

Normally when this stage is reached the dressing of the fly is complete, but as a further aid to clarity only a few turns of thread have been laid on the shank. When the head of the fly has been built, hold the thread in the left hand and place the first two fingers of the right hand on the thread.

Step 2

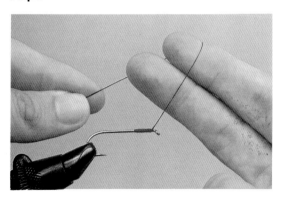

Keeping tension with the left hand, raise the fingers of the right hand above the shank, forming an open-ended loop with the thread.

Step 3

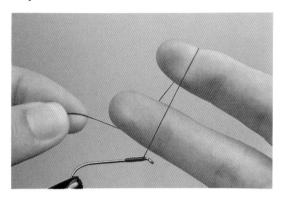

With the second – the lower – finger of the right hand, push at the end of thread held in the left.

Step 4

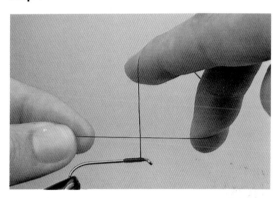

Keep pushing down with the lower finger, twisting the hand round so that the thread forms a reversed figure 4, as in the half hitch.

Step 5

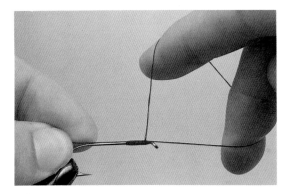

Push down further with the lower finger at the same time following it down with the left hand. This causes the bobbin holder end of the thread to lie tight along the hook shank, particularly just behind the eye of the hook.

Step 6

Keep pushing down with the second finger, taking the loop to a position below the hook shank. This carries the whipping end of the thread in a turn over the top of the hook shank and over the standing end of thread.

Step 7

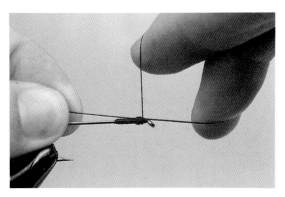

Now repeat the movement made in Step 2. Bring the fingers up above the hook shank, pushing down again with the lower finger to form the same reversed figure 4. This produces the first full turn of the whip finish and is the key to the whole exercise. Produce five full turns by repeating the previous steps four more times.

Step 8

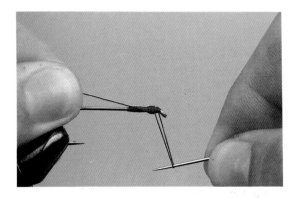

Complete the whip finish by drawing back the bobbin holder end of the thread with the left hand. This will cause the loop held in the right hand to pull tight. Whatever you do, though, do not release tension on the loop. This will allow the turns to spring off over the hook eye and destroy the whip finish. To keep tension, place a needle point in the loop once it becomes too small for the fingers to fit in.

Step 9

Finally, pull the thread tight and carefully remove the waste end of thread with a pair of scissors.

The Whip-Finish Tool

Various tools are available for creating a whip finish and whilst they all may look a bit different, most are based on two sprung metal arms connected to a handle which is twisted during the operation. The actual production of a whip-finish knot differs little, whether fingers or a special tool are used, so in this sequence the illustrations aren't quite so comprehensive. The metal arms of the tool serve simply as substitute fingers, so if you do have any difficulty you can check against the previous sequence.

Step 1

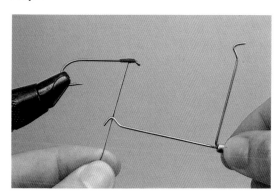

Holding the whip-finish tool in the right hand, place the arm which is in line with the handle on to the tying thread.

Step 2

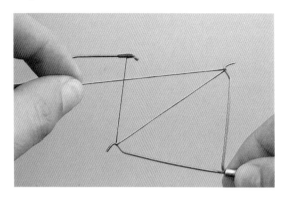

Keeping tension with the left hand, place the tying thread over the hook of the second arm, to form an inverted and reversed figure 4.

Step 3

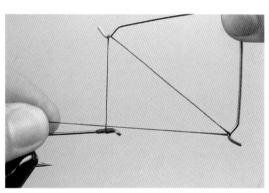

Make a 180-degree turn with the handle, bringing the reversed figure 4 of thread above the hook shank.

Step 4

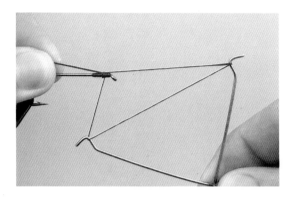

Twist the handle another 180 degrees. This will form the first turn of the whip finish.

Step 5

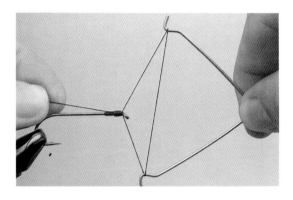

Repeat the sequence five times.

Step 6

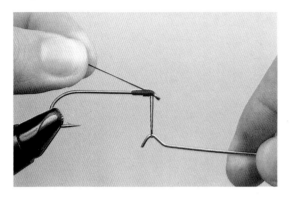

Pull the loop closed with the left hand. Remove the second arm, the one which lies at right angles to the handle, leaving the other still in the loop to keep tension until it is drawn closed.

Step 7

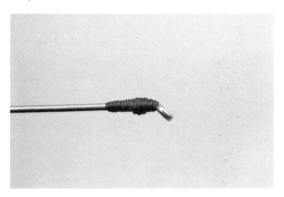

Once the whip finish has been drawn tight, remove the waste thread with a pair of scissors. The completed whip finish.

It is worthwhile spending a few hours practising the above techniques until you are reasonably proficient in them. They alter little, from the smallest of dries to the largest saltwater streamer, and time spent getting familiar with them will be time saved when actually tying.

3 Style and Proportion

The tying of a fly involves more than simply binding on a range of materials in a predetermined order. Those materials must each be applied to produce a specific effect, which varies depending on whether the pattern is a lure, a nymph or a wet or dry fly. But it is not just the materials in themselves which make each fly different. Within the rules of fly tying there are certain guidelines to proportion laid down to help the tyer achieve the result the orginator of the pattern intended. These ensure that tail, wing and hackle are of the correct dimensions, that they are neither too long nor too short, too bulky nor too sparse, allowing an individual fly to be reproduced exactly many times over. This is especially the case in those patterns described as 'traditional' — flies either wet or dry originating from the nineteenth century or before. A strict adherence to proportion resulted in flies all of a similar outline, with only the colours being different. Today the craft of fly tying is perhaps less rigid but there is still much to be said for a thorough grasp of proportion. Where the beginner is concerned it is of great importance as it is the basis for a sound tying technique and the ability to experiment with confidence.

A good illustration of why proportion is so necessary occurs when we come to tie imitative patterns. This means applying fur and feather to a hook to produce something lifelike enough to fool a trout into taking it as a natural food item. The various creatures which as fly fishers we have to imitate fall within certain well-defined groups. Best known of all are the upwinged flies, or ephemerids, of which the mayfly is a member. In order to imitate such an insect we must have some idea of its basic outline. For this reason I have included a photograph of the insect itself along with a drawing, to clarify the various points. Although the species which fall within the family Ephemeroptera vary greatly in size, at this point size doesn't matter — merely the relationship between wing and body length, the angle of the wings and where the legs are positioned. In other words, the insect's proportions. To produce an effective representation of the mayfly, or any other creature for that matter, we must replicate the most significant points in its make-up. So you can see the need for correct proportion. When tying an imitation it is no good having a wing twice the length of that of the natural, or a body which is too short and fat. The dimensions of the fly need to be the same as that of the real insect.

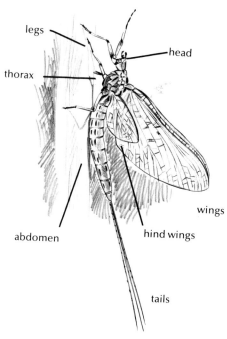

legs

head

thorax

wings

abdomen

hind wings

tails

Female, spinner or imago, of the mayfly
Ephemera danica.

Like most things in fly tying, a feel for proportion is something that is gained with experience. At first this means very much 'tying by the book'. When starting off it is good idea to get some practical help, either from a local fly-tying class or a friend who is already an experienced tyer. It is also helpful to look through books and magazines for well-respected tyers, study their work and even try to copy it. There is nothing wrong with this at all and many of the top fly tyers I know would feel flattered that someone was trying to emulate them.

Whilst the basis for the correct proportions in a fly comes from a practical desire for imitation, there is more to it than that. While members of the 'I tie flies just to catch fish' school may mock, it is still more satisfying to tie an aesthetically pleasing fly than one which is unkempt and scruffy, even if both are equally effective. This applies as much for bucktails and streamers as it does for more obviously imitative dressings such as nymphs, wet flies and dries. Throughout the

book the proportions of the flies being tied are shown in the illustrated steps, and the drawings below typify the four main categories of trout fly – wet fly, dry fly, nymph and streamer – and the traditional salmon fly, and show the positioning of the various components in relation to the hook.

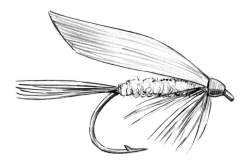

Wet fly.

Dry fly.

Nymph.

Streamer.

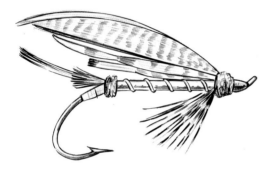

Salmon fly.

The photographs below provide a basic set of guidelines to the proportions of these five categories of fly. These will allow a beginning to be made. Further to this, the patterns shown in the illustrated tying sequences should give a guide to other types, such as spiders, parachute-hackled flies, hackle-fibre wings, and so on. Unfortunately, the written word has a tendency to be interpreted as a rule. Whilst it is a good idea, particularly for the beginner, to adhere closely to guidelines on proportion, as confidence is gained experimentation should take up a good deal of time at the vice.

A Typical Wet Fly – The Butcher

The wing   Wing length is variable. Although the traditional length is for the tips to extend slightly past the bend, most modern dressers tend towards a wing of approximately 1¼ – 1½ times the length of the hook shank. This gives a

more streamlined effect. Width should be ¾ that of the hook gape, the prepared slip being mounted a head length back from the hook eye. In the tying sequences in Chapter 8 the wing slips are always applied so that the tips curve naturally upwards. This is the traditional style but they may also be tied in with the tips swept downwards, giving a more lifelike outline to emerger patterns.

The body   This should extend from the back of the head to a point opposite the hook barb.

The rib   If there is a rib, four evenly spaced turns are usually enough.

The hackle   The fibres of the hackle should be just long enough to reach the hook point or equal the hook gape.

The tail   For feather-slip or wool tails, length should be half that of the hook shank. Hackle-fibre and other filamentous tails may be increased to as much as the same length as the hook shank.

The head   This should be the same length as the hook eye.

A Typical Dry Fly – The Red Quill

The wing   This should be twice the length of the hook gape. As the upright wing of a mayfly is

being imitated, wing width may be as much as the hook gape, though I prefer a slimmer effect.

The body This should extend back from the base of the wing to a position opposite the hook barb or just before the bend of the hook curves away. It should also taper slightly towards the tail.

The rib Where used, it should be an even spiral of four or five turns.

The hackle Length of fibre should one and a half to two times the hook gape.

The tail Tails of hackle fibre vary between one and one and a half times the length of the body, or twice the hook gape.

The head This should be the same length as the hook eye.

A Typical Nymph – The Thorax-Hackled Pheasant Tail Nymph

The abdomen The abdomen is either two-thirds or half the length of the hook shank.

The thorax Since it suggests the thorax and wing cases of the nymph, the thorax is proportional to the body and therefore takes up

either half or one-third the length of the hook shank. The difference depends on the type of insect being imitated. For example, stoneflies and the smaller mayfly species tend to have a longer thorax – half the length of the hook shank – than the larger mayflies or dragonfly and damselfly nymphs.

The rib In standard form the rib should be the same four turns as for the wet fly. On very long-shanked hooks the number of neat open turns may be increased. Also, on 'true to life' dressings, the number of turns should correspond to those of the natural.

The hackle The hackle fibres, suggesting the creature's legs, should be either the same length as the thorax or that of the hook gape.

The tail The tail is either half or one-third the length of the hook shank.

The head The same length as the hook eye.

A Typical Streamer – The Black Ghost

The wing Streamer patterns are the most variable of all fly types as far as wing length goes. It is normally one and a half to two times the length of the hook shank but, in some very mobile patterns, may be even longer.

The body   The body extends from the head back to a point opposite the hook barb.

The rib   Because of the greatly differing length of the hook shanks and width of ribbing materials used for streamers, the number of ribbing turns also varies. As a guide, for a size 6 Patridge Bucktail/Streamer hook six turns are quite adequate.

The hackle   Length should be one-third to half the length of the hook shank.

The tail   The tail should be one-third the length of the hook.

The head   In a streamer the head is usually quite pronounced, especially if it needs to accept a painted eye. From one and a half times to twice the length of the hook eye is the norm.

A Traditional Fully-Dressed Salmon Fly – The Silver Doctor

The tag   This may be in either one or two sections. Fine round or flat metal tinsel and floss are the usual materials, used singly or in combination. The tag should lie directly over the barb.

The tail   Usually of golden pheasant crest, it should be one and a half times the hook gape.

The over-tail   Length should be one-third to half that of the main tail.

The butt   The butt usually consists of three or four turns of ostrich herl, or wool teased out and dubbed for the same distance.

The body   For standard salmon dressings the body should run from the back of the head to a position opposite the hook point. For the 'low water' style of tying see the illustration of the Stoat's Tail at the end of this chapter. Occasionally the body may be formed in two or three equal sections, with each section forming half or one-third of the standard body length. If the body is sectioned, each section may be veiled above and below with lengths of feather or floss equal to that of the section.

The rib   Five open turns of tinsel form the rib. In flies for practical use, I often make the turns of tinsel in the opposite spiral to that in which the body is wound. The traditional method, however, is to wind the rib in the same direction, which allows a body hackle to be butted up against each turn of the rib.

The throat hackle   The length of the fibres should be approximately one and a half times the hook gape. Throat hackles may be either cock hackles or body hackles from various duck or other gamebird species. Often two hackles are wound at the throat, usually a cock hackle overlaid with teal, mallard or guinea-fowl.

The underwing   The underwing is made up of various materials, including golden pheasant tippet, golden pheasant tail and jungle cock. Most materials are tied in at the same length as the main wing. The two main exceptions are golden pheasant tippet and jungle cock. The former is tied in only slightly longer than the body, and the latter slightly longer than the main wing, so that the 'enamelled' eye shows clear.

The wing   The main wing, which is constructed from strips of both natural and dyed feather fibre, falls just short of the tail tip. Width is between half and two-thirds of the hook gape.

The overwing   The overwing, or roof, invariably consists of strips of bronze mallard or, on very large dressings, brown mottled turkey. Width should be approximately half that of the main wing.

The sides   These sides are usually of duck flank such as teal and wood duck, either used singly or in strips married together. Length should be one-third to half the length of the main wing. If jungle cock cheeks are used they should be half to three-quarters the length of the sides.

The topping   Normally of golden pheasant topping, it should reach the very tip of the tail.

The head   If simply of thread, it should be the same length as the eye; if wool is used, it should be slightly longer.

Fly tying is not an exact science and is therefore open to much experimentation and development. Closely linked to proportion is style. Even though every dressing comprises a fixed list of materials, each tied in a specific way, many experienced tyers have an individual style which sets their work apart. Style is something which is difficult to define but is connected with the way in which each angler uses a pattern. An example of this would be a fly such as the Soldier Palmer.

This bushy palmered fly is tremendously effective on the lakes, lochs and loughs of England, Scotland and Ireland. Dressed large, with plenty of hackle, it works extremely well in rough conditions when the water's surface is moving to a good wave.

Now many of the heavily-dressed traditional patterns such as the Soldier Palmer are considered to be most effective during a big wind. The only trouble with traditions is that they can perpetuate myths. Anglers fishing on the English lowland stillwaters found that the Soldier Palmer could be just as effective in very calm conditions, provided that the style of tying was altered. Instead of the thick, bulky body and heavy palmering, the fly was tied with a finely-dubbed body and a sparse body hackle. Some anglers even tied a range of Soldier Palmers from the heavy hackled versions for rough conditions, through others for normal weather, to the ultrafine dressings for calm water. What many found, though, was that even in a big wave the finer dressings were often the more effective. This in turn resulted in a basic change in the style in which the Soldier Palmer is tied, at least by those fishing the Midland and Southern reservoirs.

This is perhaps a simplistic example, since individual style is rather more subtle than this, but I hope it illustrates the point. Over recent years there has been a definite move away from the heavy 'traditional' style of tying towards much sparser patterns. Patterns ranging from nymphs and dry flies to salmon and sea-trout dressings have all undergone the same change and increased in effectiveness as a consequence. The main thing when tying any pattern is to consider where and how it is to be fished. Being able to adapt your style to individual dressings is something that will come with practice. As a guide, the photographs on pages 30 and 31 show a small range of patterns dressed in a variety of styles. In each, the materials used are the same and only the amounts vary.

The Peter Ross – A Standard Wet Fly

The fly tied full with high-angled wing for fishing swiftly-flowing rivers.

The slimline version with sparse hackle and low wing for slow-moving or stillwater.

The Soldier Palmer – A Traditional Loch-Style Dressing

Tied full for a heavy wave.

Normal tying for a gentle breeze.

Tied sparse for calm conditions, or when the water is particularly clear.

The Stoat's Tail – A Popular Hairwing Salmon Fly

Tied short and sparse, 'low water' style. Effective during the summer period when the river is showing its bare bones.

The normal dressing tied on a standard-weight salmon iron.

4 Tails

The tail of a fly can fulfil a number of purposes. In imitative dressings it can suggest the setae of the natural insect as well as providing balance in a floating fly. In general attractors the addition of a tail can give an all-important flash of colour, transforming a good pattern into a real killer. Tails can even be used as extensions or even substitutes for a wing – consider the example of the Dog Nobbler or Crappie Jig, where the whole action of the fly is based on a long pulsating tail.

The range of materials used for tails is vast, but as most are actually applied in a very similar manner, a few specific examples will suffice to illustrate the techniques.

Wool Tails

Simplest of all are tails made from wool. They consist of a small tag of wool, often bright red in colour, which when wet provides a wonderful succulent effect to the end of a fly. Interestingly, the red wool tail is often used as a bright point contrasting with the more sombre colours of patterns such as the Red Tag and Zulu.

Fluorescents, too, play their part. Many traditional patterns have been enhanced by the addition of a tail of fluorescent wool, even those which didn't have a tail in the first place. Yellow and green are the most effective colours, particularly during mid-season, though bright orange and pink also work well.

The method used to produce a wool tail works equally well with other materials, including floss and various yarns, and whatever the type of wool used, the tying method is much the same. The dressing used to illustrate the sequence, the Woolly Worm, is a grand bottom-grubbing pattern. With its juicy chenille body and palmered hackle it can be tied in a wide range of colours and sizes and is therefore great for suggesting most aquatic creatures, from shrimps to dragonfly nymphs. Here the dressing is a simple green with a grizzle hackle and a red wool tag, though body and hackle colour may be altered to suit.

Step 1

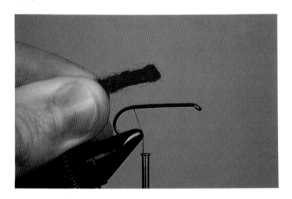

Select a size 10 longshank nymph hook and after fixing it in the vice run on a length of black tying thread down to the bend. Select a piece of red wool approximately 1 inch in length. When tying larger patterns you can use the wool straight from the ball, but with smaller hooks, untwist the yarn and use just one strand to keep the tail in proportion to the rest of the fly.

Step 2

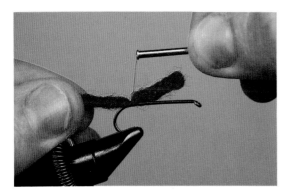

Hold the length of wool above the hook and catch it in at the bend with three tight turns of thread. Make sure that half the length projects from the rear of the hook, with the remainder lying along the shank.

Step 3

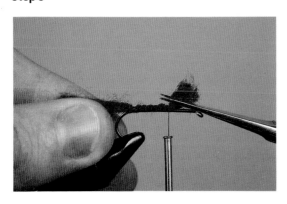

Take the thread back up the shank towards the eye, binding down the wool, and remove the excess with a pair of scissors. I prefer to keep the waste end of tail materials running along the hook shank just so long as they don't create too much bulk. Doing this ensures that the body is kept even and helps prevent unsightly tail-end bumps.

Step 4

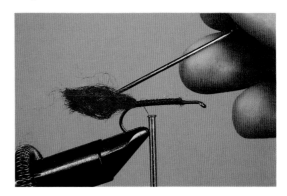

Run the thread back down to the tail in tight touching turns then, with a dubbing needle, tease out all the fibres of the wool tail until they become quite fluffy.

Step 5

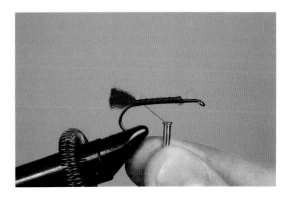

That done, clip the tail to length, in this case ¼ inch, though it will vary depending on the size of hook used. With the tail complete you are now ready to add the remainder of the materials, which comprise a length of olive-green chenille and a grizzle hackle.

Step 6

The finished Woolly Worm.

To prevent the pictures in each sequence from becoming repetitive only those necessary to the technique being illustrated are given. In this and most other instances the methods required to complete the fly are shown in more relevant chapters, the palmered hackle in Chapter 7 and the chenille body in Chapter 5. In this way it should be possible to take information from each chapter, adding together the required parts to build a comprehensive range of patterns.

Hackle-Fibre Tails

If not the most easy to tie then certainly the most often-used tail type is that made from hackle fibres. Because hackle fibres are cheap and readily available, in a wide variety of natural and dyed colours, they work equally well in patterns as diverse as large saltwater lures and the tiniest dry fly. It is as dry-fly and wet-fly tails that they are most useful, though, imitating the tail filaments of the natural insect as well as providing stability and floatability in dry patterns.

A good example of a standard hackle-fibre tail comes in the Red Quill. A superb 'banker' pattern, the Red Quill is a simple hackled fly, tied in both wet and dry versions and effective on lake and stream when the fish are taking small ephemerids. In this instance the dry Red Quill is illustrated, dressed on a size 14 Hooper down-eyed dry-fly hook.

Step 1

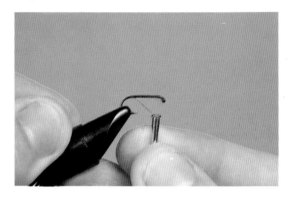

Fix the hook in the vice and run on a length of pre-waxed brown tying thread to the bend.

Step 2

Select a bright, stiff-fibred, natural red cock hackle. You will find that the spade-shaped feathers on the very edges of the cape provide the most suitable fibres. (For wet flies and streamers, feathers from any part of the cape may be used.) With index finger and thumb, stroke out the fibres several times so they lie at right angles to the hackle stalk. This ensures that all the tips are even.

Step 3

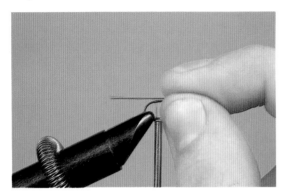

If all the fibres seem perfect, with no crinkling or broken tips, gently tear away a small bunch. For a fly of this size, five or six fibres will be about right. Also, tearing off the fibres, rather than cutting, helps to keep the bunch together. Offer the bunch up to the hook shank so that the tips project over the bend. The length does vary but in traditional patterns such as the Red Quill a tail just slightly longer than the hook shank is ideal.

Step 4

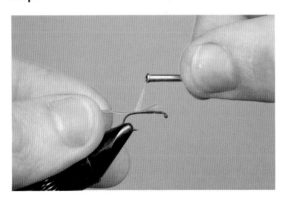

Holding the bunch in position, take three tight turns over the butts. Ensure that the bunch lies in line with the hook shank, without any definite downward slant.

Step 5

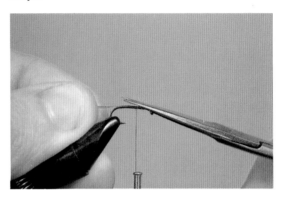

Continue the thread two-thirds of the way up the shank, covering the butts. Remove the excess hackle fibre with a pair of scissors. With the tail now complete the thread should be wound back down to the bend to finish off the dressing. With the modern nylon threads which spread flat this process doesn't create too much bulk; indeed, it gives a good solid foundation for the body materials.

Step 6

The Red Quill. *See* Chapters 5 and 7 for the remainder of the dressing.

V Tails

As a supplement to the standard hackle-fibre tail, the V tail is specific to the dry fly, notably the lightly hackled or no-hackle spent patterns. Here the well-spread tail filaments assist the fly in floating right in the surface film. The initial stages of tying this type of tail are the same as for the previous technique. Fine stiff hair can also be used in the same fashion.

Step 1

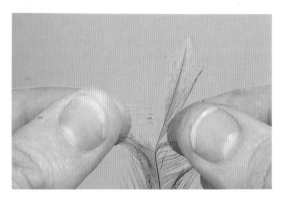

After preparing a size 14 Captain Hamilton dry-fly hook for dressing, select a spade hackle from a blue dun cock cape. (Although blue dun is used here, select the correct colour to suit the pattern you are tying.) After stroking out the fibres tear off six or eight. In very small patterns, especially if they are to be fished in flat or still conditions, as few as two or four fibres may be used.

Step 2

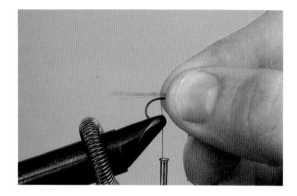

Judge the tail for length.

Step 3

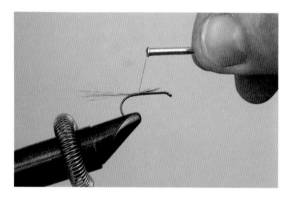

Secure the tail with a few turns of thread.

Step 4

That done, gently divide the fibres into two equal bunches so each lies at approximately 30 degrees either side of the hook shank. This V-split is kept in place by figure-of-eight turns of thread run through the base of the hackle fibres.

Step 5

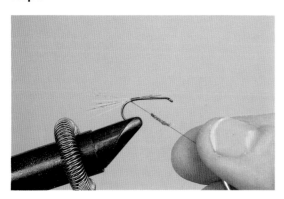

As a further aid to keeping the two bunches of fibres apart, a small pinch of dubbing material is spun on the thread and formed into a tiny ball wound in between the bunches.

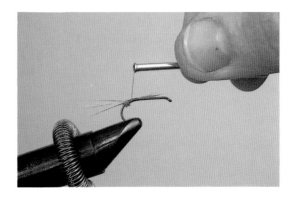

Wind the dubbing ball between the tail filaments, then take the tying thread back to the tail base before dubbing the rest of the body.

Step 6

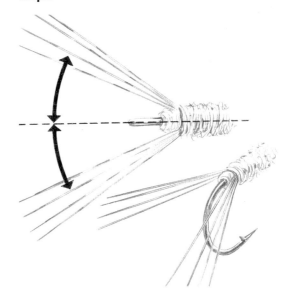

The position of the dubbing ball is in relation to the tails and the angle of set of the tails.

Step 7

Tail complete, the remainder of the dressing may be continued. In this case it is simply a body of rusty brown Superla dubbing and a thorax hackle of blue dun cock, trimmed top and bottom to form wings. *See* Chapters 5 and 7.

Step 8

The Hackle Spinner.

Wood Duck Tails

Wood duck, or summer duck as it is often known, is a beautiful feather taken from the flank of the drake Carolina wood duck. It is available both barred and plain, the barring being a wonderfully vibrant black and white. Both forms are based on a lemon colour flecked with black. The illustrated tying sequence deals with the latter, though the technique is just as applicable to other types of duck flank tails such as teal or pintail, as well as golden pheasant tippet, pheasant tail and other gamebird feathers.

Step 1

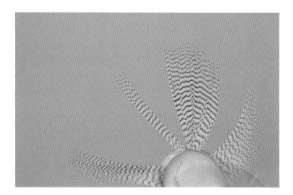

Select a well-marked wood duck flank feather. Ensure that it is a nice clean lemon colour and that the fibres are even and unbroken. Remove a slip containing eight to ten fibres.

Step 2

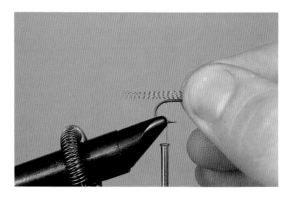

Take a standard wet-fly hook, in this instance a size 12 Captain Hamilton medium-weight, and run a length of pre-waxed brown tying thread down from the eye to the end of the hook shank. This is the standard tail position for most flies. Hold the slip of wood duck above the hook and judge for length. Here the tips of wood duck should project back about the same distance as the length of the hook shank.

Step 3

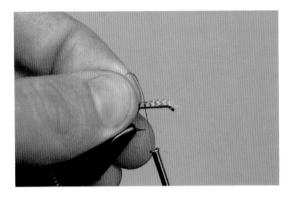

Once you are happy with the length, switch hands, holding the slip very close to the hook. Make one loose and open turn of thread over the fibres, keeping tension off the thread until the bobbin holder is directly below the hook. Then pull down steadily on the thread, drawing it tightly over the fibres. This technique, which locks the tail in place, is known as a 'winging loop' and is equally useful for both tails and wings, and indeed for any material which must be kept on top of the hook shank. Basically it counteracts the sideward pull caused by winding the thread in the normal manner, an action which will pull any material with it and out of position and is the cause of many a twisted tail or useless wing. I make no apologies for referring to the winging loop throughout the book. The drawing shows it in greater detail.

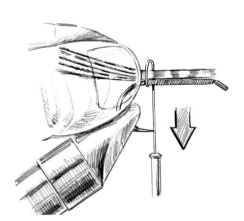

Step 4

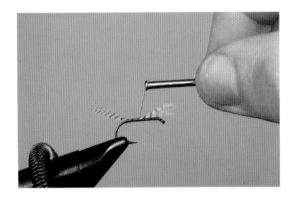

With the tail in position, wind further turns of thread over the butts to secure.

Step 5

With a material as fine as wood duck I prefer to take the thread well up the hook shank before trimming off the waste. Doing so creates negligible bulk and provides a very even underbody.

Step 6

Tail complete, carry on the dressing. In the illustration it is of the Light Cahill, a good imitation of the more colourful mayfly species. It is tied with a body of cream fur, a light-ginger hackle and a wing also of lemon wood duck.

Paired Slip Tails

Probably best known as the tailing method for the Muddler Minnow, paired slip tails work well for many streamer and wet-fly patterns. Goose, duck and turkey are the standard materials, being strongly webbed and robust. The technique involves placing together matched slips of feather in the same manner as the paired slip wing (*see* Chapter 8). Here the pattern illustrated is the Muddler Minnow.

Step 1

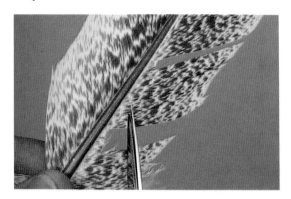

Take a pair of mottled turkey quills and from each remove a slip of the same size. Though the exact number will vary depending on the hook used, here eight to ten fibres in each slip is about right.

Step 2

Fix a size 10 Partridge Captain Hamilton Nymph hook in the vice and run on brown tying thread from eye to bend. The prepared tail slips are also shown.

Step 3

Place the turkey slips dull sides out, ensuring that the tips are even. Hold the prepared tail over the hook shank to judge for length. In this case the tail should be a third to half the length of the hook.

Step 4

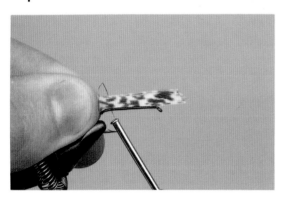

Transfer your grip on the tail to the other hand and catch it in place with a winging loop.

Step 5

Make two further turns of thread to secure the tail in position. Continue the tying thread up the hook, covering the tail butts before trimming off the waste.

Step 6

Complete the dressing with a body of flat gold ribbed with wire, a wing of grey squirrel overlaid with mottled turkey, all finished off with a head of spun and clipped deer hair.

Golden Pheasant Crest Tails

This lovely translucent yellow feather taken from the crest of the golden pheasant provides the mainstay for tailing salmon flies as well as many patterns of wet fly for both trout and sea trout. For the tying sequence I have used the Stinchar

Stoat's Tail, an extremely popular and effective hairwing salmon fly.

Step 1

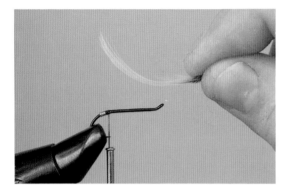

Fix a size 6 loop-eyed Partridge salmon hook in the vice. Run black tying thread from the eye down the shank to a point slightly round the bend. Here catch in 2 inches of fine round silver tinsel. With the tinsel, make six tightly-butted turns to form a tag, taking the thread back up to the tail position. Select a brightly-coloured golden pheasant crest feather. The best are not only a rich golden hue but have a deep-orange tip to them. The curve should be gentle and not too pronounced.

Step 2

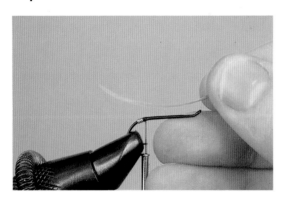

If the curve is wrong or the feather twisted (as it often is during the curing process), this can be remedied by wetting and allowing the feather to dry in a different set. A piece of glass is very useful for this, and at a pinch you can even use the window next to your tying bench. Whilst wet, the crest can be formed into a more desirable curve and using a flat piece of glass ensures that the centre stem is kept on an even plane. Once prepared, judge the tail for length.

Step 3

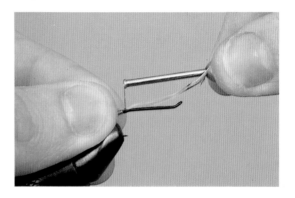

Catch the crest in with two turns of thread.

Step 4

Continue winding the thread over the crest feather, trimming off the waste further down the shank.

Step 5

Complete the Stinchar Stoat's Tail with a body of black floss ribbed with oval silver tinsel, an orange cock hackle and a wing of black stoat's tail, or black squirrel tail as a substitute.

Hair Tails

Hair tails are useful on both bucktails and streamers as well as on some of the larger dry-fly patterns, including the Wulff series. Many types of hair can be used, including squirrel and calf, though for dry flies the buoyancy of bucktail makes it the first choice.

Step 1

From a natural brown bucktail cut away a generous bunch of hair.

Step 2

Prepare the tail by removing all the soft base hairs and those with broken tips.

Step 3

If the tips are very uneven they may be lined up by 'stacking' the hair. This may be accomplished by first holding the bunch loosely between fingers and thumb, slightly above a hard flat surface. Jiggle the hairs between your fingers and gravity will cause them to drop until they touch the flat surface.

Step 4

With the tail prepared, offer it up to the hook.

Step 5

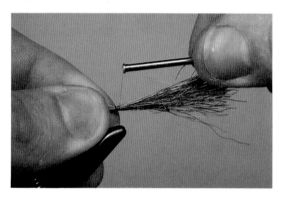

Holding the bunch in position, take three or four tight turns of thread round the base.

Step 6

To further secure the tail in place, work a few drops of varnish into the hair butts before covering them with tight turns of thread.

Step 7

Trim off the waste.

Step 8

Complete the dressing, which in this case is the Irresistible dry fly, by adding a wing of brown bucktail, a dark-grey cock hackle and a body of spun and clipped deer hair. This pattern is extremely buoyant, which makes it superb for very rough water.

The Marabou Tail

Marabou is a fantastic material. Its wonderful mobility when wet makes it ideal for a wide range of patterns, from general attractors and fry imitations to wet flies and nymphs. But, like so many materials today, marabou is not what it seems. Originally obtained from the Marabou stork, hence the name, marabou now comes from between the legs of the white domestic turkey. The substitute lacks none of the required properties and a generous tuft of marabou as a tail gives a sinuous action to any tying, especially the lead-head dressings which have taken the trout-fishing world by storm over recent years. Patterns such as the Dog Nobbler, Frog Nobbler and Puppy lures, all based on lead-head jigs, have proved extremely effective on all types of stillwater. In running water, flies for migratory trout and salmon have all benefited from the addition of marabou.

Not all patterns based on Crappie lures and lead-head jigs need to be lures, though. Marabou's beautiful action lends itself just as well to more imitative patterns, notably those where the natural is very active. For this reason I have chosen the marabou-tailed damsel nymph for the tying sequence. I know that the damselfly nymph is not generally regarded as an exceptionally nippy creature, preferring instead to spend most of its existence well camouflaged in a weed bed. But when it wants to put on a turn of speed it is a mean mover, propelling itself with rapid swishing of the abdomen. With this in mind the action of marabou provides an admirable and effective imitation.

Step 1

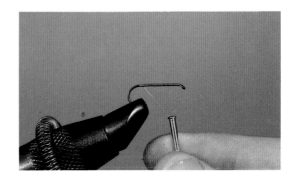

Fix a size 10 Captain Hamilton Nymph hook in the vice and run on a length of olive tying thread to the bend.

Step 2

From a marabou plume remove a generous bunch of fibres.

Step 3

Offer the bunch up to the hook, judging for length. There is no real perfect length here but as a guideline it should be approximately twice that of the hook shank.

Step 4

Catch the bunch in with two turns of thread. The actual density of the bunch can be varied. In more imitative dressings I prefer to keep it relatively light, as in the illustration, whilst for the larger lures larger, denser tails may be employed.

Step 5

Run the tying thread back up the hook shank, binding down the marabou butts securely. Keeping the waste feather running the length of the hook prevents any unevenness in the body.

Step 6

Stop the thread two-thirds of the way along the shank and trim off the excess material.

Step 7

Complete the tying by adding lead eyes varnished black (*see* Chapter 9), a body of the same olive marabou dubbed on and ribbed with gold, plus a few fibres of brown partridge as a throat hackle. The Marabou Damselfly Nymph.

Tails don't have to be brightly coloured to be effective.

5 Bodies

The tying of a strong, sound body is the key to good fly-dressing technique. It provides the base to all the other components and if both strength and proportion aren't right the addition of hackle or wing will be made all the more difficult.

Though invariably a 'fixed' part of the fly, the body, through careful use of materials, may be used to express a wide range of properties. These can vary enormously, depending on the application. For instance, in coloured or fast-moving water, where the fly might need to be highly visible, a strong outline is called for. Floss, chenille and wool all offer the right amount of bulk, and are quickly applied even on large hooks. Extra sparkle may come from metallic substances such as metal tinsels, Mylar piping (ideal for fish imitations), or one of the other metallised plastics, which have the added bonus of being tarnish-resistant and so retain their shine indefinitely.

In the other extreme, the body can exhibit delicate translucence, so much the mark of contemporary nymphs and dry flies, patterns used to fool educated trout in crystal-clear waters. Feather fibre, herl, seal fur, not forgetting the vast array of man-made dubbing materials, in single colours and blends, go together to provide the fly dresser with possibilities limited only by his imagination.

Beginning with peacock herl, a basic but highly effective material, this chapter covers all the major contemporary techniques.

Peacock Herl

Bronze peacock herl is perhaps the most widely used body material and is one of the easiest to handle. Its fluffy, sparkling effect is incorporated in killing patterns world-wide, both as wet and dry fly, attractor and imitation. Its lightness yet apparent bulk make it ideal for beetle and other terrestrial imitations, though with the addition of weight it makes superb early-season bottom-grubbing dressings, including caddis larvae and the Black and Peacock Spider, and I have chosen the latter to illustrate the technique.

Step 1

Size of hook may be varied but I prefer a size 12 Partridge Captain Hamilton. After fixing it securely in the vice run on a length of black tying thread, finishing up at the bend. Take a peacock tail feather and after pulling the fibres out straight remove six to eight fibres.

Step 2

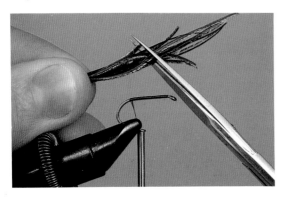

Even so, it is difficult to get all the tips even, so the best method is to trim them flush.

Step 3

Catch the points in at the bend with two turns of thread. Leave the tips lying along the length of the shank to prevent a bulge occurring at the tail end.

Step 4

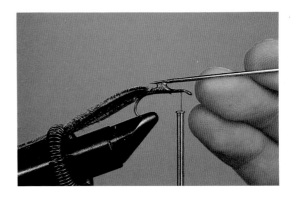

Wind the thread up the hook, covering the tips, to a point just short of the eye. Then, using a dubbing needle, coat the shank liberally with lacquer.

Step 5

As the lacquer dries and becomes tacky, twist the herl gently to form a fuzzy rope and wind it up the shank towards the eye.

Step 6

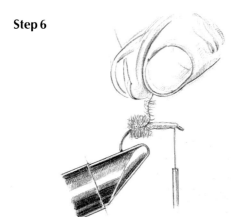

As you wind the rope up the shank, continue to twist it in a clockwise direction between finger and thumb.

Step 7

Catch in the waste ends with two turns of thread.

Step 8

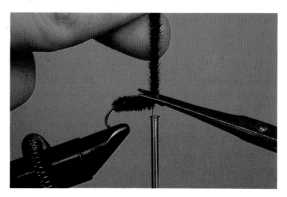

Trim off the waste ends and leave to dry for a few moments. The lacquer will soak into the herl rope and when dry will stick the herls securely to the hook shank, producing a more robust body than a rib.

Step 9

The completed Black and Peacock Spider. This is only one of many combinations. Different types of hackle may be used, including badger, grizzle, and natural red game. Tails of wool, golden pheasant tippets, and so on, add another whole new dimension. Peacock herl also makes superb thoraxes for midge pupa imitations as well as abdominal gills for ephemerid nymphs. The possibilities are almost limitless.

Feather Fibre

One of the most useful and adaptable body materials, particularly for imitative patterns, is feather fibre. The fibre can come from a variety of sources. White goose is especially useful as it can be dyed in a wide array of colours and shades to match the body coloration of any nymph or adult insect. In nymphal patterns the tiny fibres running in the length of each feather fibre work in the water, providing just the right combination of translucency and movement so vital in a slowly-fished fly.

Of all the feather-fibre-bodied patterns certainly the best known is the Pheasant Tail Nymph, tied from the tail fibres of a pheasant – to be precise, the rich chestnut tails of the male bird. Not strictly an imitative pattern, more a suggestion of something living and edible, the Pheasant Tail Nymph catches on river and stillwater alike. Whilst the colours used in feather-fibre nymphs and flies vary, the method of dressing does not, and to illustrate it I use the ubiquitous Pheasant Tail Nymph, the materials for which are both cheap and easy to obtain.

Since it suggests so many creatures, both large and small, the Pheasant Tail Nymph can be dressed on hooks ranging from a diminutive 18 to a longshank 6, depending on the application. I have stuck to middle ground with a 12 longshank, a size which is not only very useful but also shows the steps more clearly than a very tiny dressing.

Step 1

The first task is to choose the required pheasant tail. The ideal is one with good, clean fibres, bright chestnut in colour. Pull six or eight fibres out at right angles to the tail shaft to bring the tips to the same length. Remove the straightened fibres at the butts.

Step 2

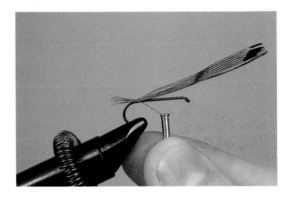

After fixing the hook in the vice run a length of brown tying thread down to the bend. There catch in the pheasant tail fibres with two turns. Allow the tips to project as tails for approximately half the length of the hook shank. At the same point catch in 3 inches of copper wire. This will form the rib and give additional weight.

Step 3

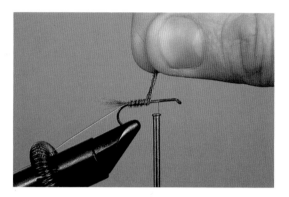

Run the tying thread two-thirds of the way back towards the eye. Then, grasping the butts of the fibres between finger and thumb, wind them in neat touching turns to the thread.

Step 4

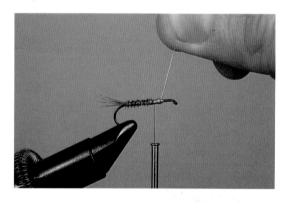

After tying down the fibres, wind the copper wire up the body in the opposite spiral. This ensures that the rib traps and protects the body fibres properly. Six open turns should be ample. If you require extra weight in the nymph use close turns of copper wire to build up a bulbous thorax.

Step 5

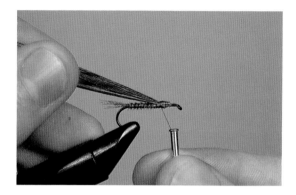

The wing cases are formed by a dozen fibres caught in by the tips.

Step 6

That done, catch in another six fibres, again by the tips, and wind them over the turns of copper wire to form the completed thorax.

Step 7

The final step is to stretch the remaining fibres over the thorax, forming the wing cases, then trim off the excess, whip finish and give a couple of coats of clear varnish to the head.

Step 8

The completed Pheasant Tail Nymph. For smaller hooks, scale down the materials accordingly.

Chenille

For larger nymphs and many lure patterns chenille has the advantage of being cheap and simple to apply. It provides the required bulk in only a few turns. When wet, chenille sinks fast as well as looking very succulent – perfect for caddis larva and stonefly nymph imitations, along with many of the bigger weighted nymphs widely used for stalking clearwater trout.

I have used one such pattern to illustrate the tying sequence. It is the Montana Nymph, an American pattern which has had great success on the British stillwater scene. Hook is a longshank from size 6 to size 12, a Captain Hamilton nymph pattern being ideal for the task.

Step 1

Fix a hook in the vice and run a length of black tying thread from eye to bend. There catch in a bunch of black cock hackle fibres, allowing the points to project as a tail for approximately one-third the length of the shank. The original demands crow feather fibre but hackle fibres are just as effective.

Step 2

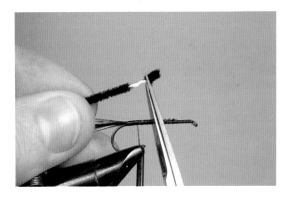

Next, take 3 inches of black chenille and remove the 'herl' from the central core. Doing this reduces bulk at the tail end, preventing an unsightly bulge. In the illustration I have used suede chenille as it is a little more robust. Whichever type of chenille is used the technique is the same.

Step 3

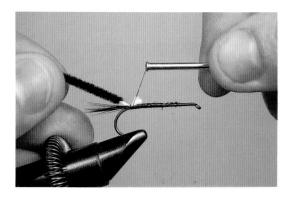

Catch in the exposed core of the chenille at the bend of the hook. Wind the tying thread two-thirds of the way back along the hook shank.

Step 4

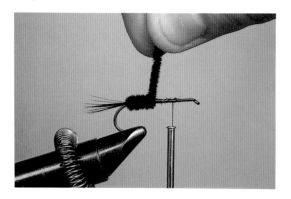

Take hold of the chenille and wind it along the hook shank in neat butted turns to where the thread has been left. Catch it in and trim off the waste.

Step 5

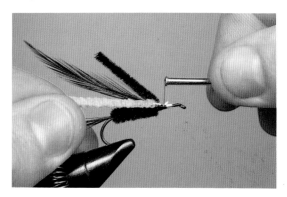

That done, in this order and all at the same point, catch in 1 inch of black chenille, a black cock hackle and 2 inches of yellow chenille. These will all go together to suggest the wing cases, legs and thorax.

Step 6

Take hold of the yellow chenille and wind it to a point just short of the eye. Catch it in and trim off the waste.

Step 7

Wind the hackle over the thorax in open turns, then stretch the black chenille over the back, catching the loose end in at the eye. Remove the excess and complete with a whip finish and two coats of black varnish.

Step 8

The Montana Nymph. If extra weight is required a little lead foil or wire may be added before commencing dressing (*see* Chapter 9).

Wool

Wool comes in a wide range of forms, from man-made fibres such as nylon to lamb's, and coarser, sheep's wool. I even have some spun from the coat of an Old English Sheepdog! The beauty of wool is its wide range of colours and the fact that it can be picked out easily to produce a wonderful 'buggy' effect. Because of its ability to take a dye it can be produced in a vast range of colours and shades, including the fluorescents which have made such an impact on latter-day trout fishing. My favourite wool is angora, a lovely soft material spun from the fleece of the angora goat. It can be obtained in a variety of colours but I prefer to buy it bleached white and dye it as I want. It is also cheaper that way.

Angora is also the material used in the best mayfly nymph imitation of them all, the Walker Mayfly Nymph, which is the pattern used in the picture sequence. It is not a very easy dressing, but is more time-consuming than taxing, and the effort is well worthwhile.

The colour of the wool used is a pale ivory, produced by dunking the wool in the merest wash of a lemon dye. Fortunately, over recent years the colour has become available commercially.

Richard Walker originally devised this nymph as a heavily weighted pattern for fishing in deep pools and for intercepting cruising fish, so the first step is to construct the lead foil underbody. This is dealt with in Chapter 9, so we will move straight on to the next stage.

Step 1

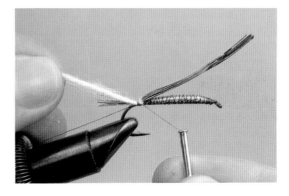

Fix in the vice a prepared lead underbody. For the Walker Mayfly Nymph this should be on a size 8 or 10 Captain Hamilton Nymph hook. Run a length of brown tying thread on to the bend, leaving the waste end, which will later form the rib. There catch in six fibres of cock pheasant tail and 3 inches of angora wool dyed palest ivory. The points of the pheasant tail fibres form the setae of the nymph.

Step 2

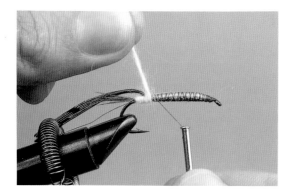

Take hold of the wool and wind two full turns over the pheasant tail butts. Lift the butts up and wind a further two turns of angora and catch it in.

Step 3

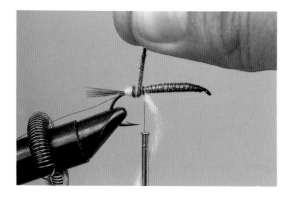

Grasp the butts of the pheasant tail fibres, give them a slight twist, and wind them in two open turns over the angora wool. These imitate the dark markings on the abdomen of the natural. Catch in and trim off the waste.

Step 4

Continue winding the wool two-thirds the way up the hook shank, tie it in and cut away the surplus.

Step 5

From the bend wind the waste end of the tying thread over the wool in a neat, open and opposite spiral. Winding the thread in the opposite direction prevents it from bedding too deeply into the wool.

Step 6

Select from fourteen to twenty cock pheasant tail fibres and, after levelling all the tips, catch the bunch in by the butts so that it projects back over the body for *twice* the length of the thorax. Catch in 2 inches of angora and form a neat thorax before trimming off the excess.

Step 7

Stretch the pheasant tail fibres over the thorax in the normal wing-case style and catch in firmly. Then divide the projecting tips into two equal bunches, binding each to either side of the thorax. This forms two sets of legs which should lie along the sides of the body slightly longer than the thorax. The drawing gives an overhead view of this job half completed. Finish off the head in the usual way.

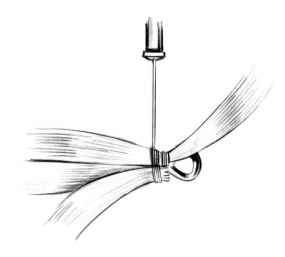

Step 8

With a dubbing needle, gently pick out the angora wool running the length of the abdomen. The intention is to suggest the diaphanous gills of the natural, a known and effective recognition point. If necessary, trim the gills to shape, taking care not to cut any of the legs.

Step 9

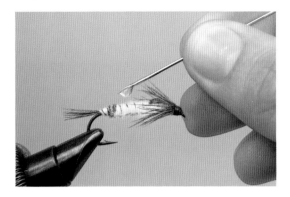

To complete, run a few drops of varnish along the top and bottom of the abdomen as well as the head. Allow it to soak in and dry before adding further coats. Doing so makes the pattern incredibly robust and you will be amazed just how many fish you can catch before a nymph is destroyed.

Step 10

The Walker Mayfly Nymph.

Simple Dubbing

As a technique for producing superb bodies for imitative patterns, dubbing has to come top of the list. Although some of the plastics outwardly look more natural, when it actually comes to fooling the fish the dubbed body is unbeatable. The beauty of dubbing is that it is so versatile: it can suggest the delicate translucence of the smallest ephemerid as well as the rugged buggy appearance of giant dragonfly or stonefly nymphs.

Many types of material may be dubbed, from simple knitting wool to various furs and man-made yarns; even marabou feather can be pressed into service, making beautiful nymph bodies. The simplest and easiest type of dubbing is where a relatively coarse fibre such as hare or seal fur is applied to a single strand of thread. A typical example of this is the Cased Caddis, a pattern from the Bob Carnill stable which works well fished deep early in the season. It is dressed on a size 10 or 12 longshank with an optional under-body of lead wire.

Step 1

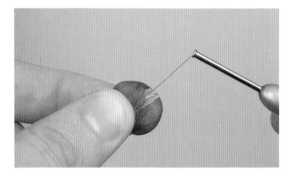

Whatever the type of dubbing, the first thing to do is ensure that the thread is well waxed. It is this waxing which helps the fibres adhere to the thread. To wax the thread, draw it a number of times through a lump of beeswax. Remember on each draw to keep the thread moving in one swift steady action. The friction melts the wax and coats the thread. An uneven action will merely cause the thread to break.

Step 2

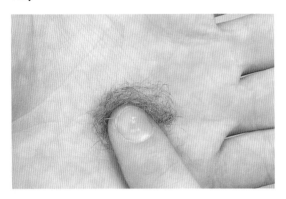

Next, prepare the dubbing material, which in this case is hare fur. From the mask of a hare pull away a few tufts of underfur together with the stiffer guard hairs. Place the fur in the palm of the hand and with the forefinger mix up the fibres. This is a very good procedure, particularly with processed hair such as seal fur, where the fibres often all lie in the same direction, which makes dubbing difficult.

Step 3

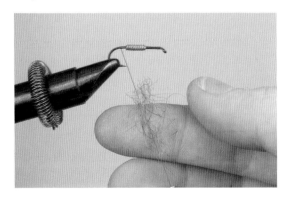

After preparing the hook with an underbody of lead wire, run the thread down to the bend. Next, take a small pinch of the prepared fur and offer it up to the waxed thread.

Step 4

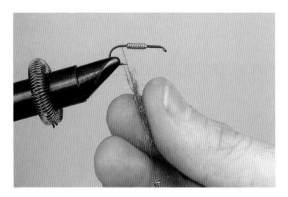

Between finger and thumb roll the fur so that it binds to the thread. Keep rolling in one direction only, or you will only unbind the fur. Do not try to dub too much fur at a time; little and often is very apt here.

Step 5

Keep adding fur until a neat tapered rope is formed.

Step 6

That done, wind the rope over the hook, covering the lead underbody. To make the body more robust you can coat the hook shank with varnish before winding. If there is not enough rope simply add more fur.

Step 7

From the finished body you can see why the guard hairs were included in the dubbing mix. They stick out from the body, producing a wonderful buggy effect. If you feel it is still not ragged enough, pick out more fibres with a dubbing needle.

Step 8

Complete the pattern by adding a thorax of white goose herl and a black cock hackle. The Cased Caddis.

The Dubbing Loop

A second method of applying a dubbed body is the dubbing loop. Its main advantage over the simple single-strand technique is that it is more adaptable, able to produce either a very tight, fine effect for dries or a looser texture for nymphs and bugs. Because it is formed with two strands of thread it is also very robust, even without being ribbed.

In the illustrated sequence the fly is a Compara Spinner tied on a size 14 Hooper dry-fly hook.

Step 1

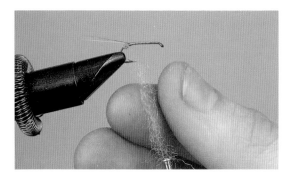

After running on a length of olive tying thread, produce a V tail as described in Chapter 4. Next prepare a small pinch of buff Superla dubbing, offering it up to the pre-waxed thread.

Step 2

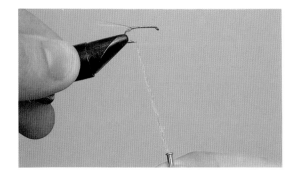

With a clockwise twist produce a finely-dubbed rope.

Step 3

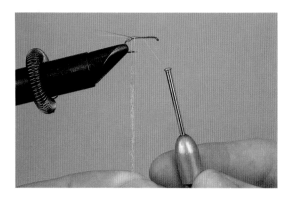

Take the tying thread back up to the hook shank and make three turns at the very point where it originally left the hook. This forms the loop.

Step 4

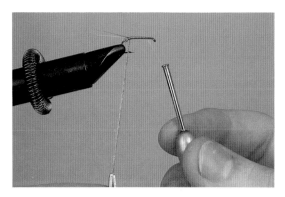

Holding the very end of the loop, begin to twist. This can be done either with a special tool which is available or with a pair of hackle pliers. As you can see from the photograph, I prefer the latter. The amount of twist depends on the effect you require. Keeping a light twist as the body is wound produces a more open, fluffy effect.

Step 5

Twisting the loop tightly, as in the illustration, produces a harder outline, even to the point of showing segmentation. Also, the tighter the loop is twisted, the more the dubbing is compacted and the thread shows through. In this case the olive colour of the thread enhances that of the dubbing.

Step 6

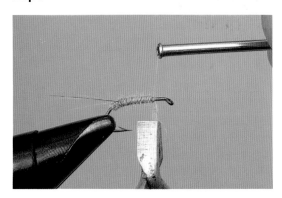

Finish the body three-quarters of the way along the hook shank, catching in and removing the excess loop.

Step 7

Complete the dressing by winding a blue dun cock hackle at the thorax before dividing the fibres into a spent-wing configuration with figure-of-eight turns of thread. Cover the turns with a dubbed thorax of the same buff Superla.

Polythene Bodies

Clear polythene has long been used when a virtually 'see through' effect is required. Shrimps and small bait-fish imitations are prime examples, where the naturals are all but transparent. Here the Polystickle, an invention of the late Richard Walker, shows the steps in tying a simple polythene body.

Step 1

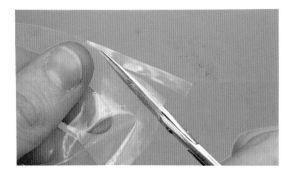

From a strip of clear polythene cut a strip approximately 4 inches long and ¼ inch wide.

Step 2

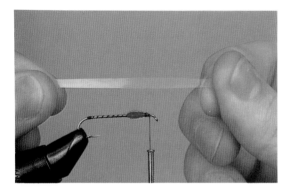

Prepare the hook by running a length of black tying thread on at the *bend* of a size 8 silvered longshank, winding it in open turns to just short of the eye. There catch in a short piece of red wool or floss and form a small thorax. This will imitate the internal organs of the small fish. Then take hold of the polythene strip and give it a good stretch. Stretching makes the polythene very clear and also allows it to be wound tightly without forever giving.

Step 3

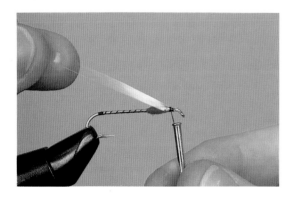

Catch the polythene strip in at the eye and begin winding it down the shank towards the bend. The intention is to create a tapered fish shape so more polythene needs to be applied to the bare shank than to the thorax. If the strip is too short to complete this, simply prepare another and add it on.

Step 4

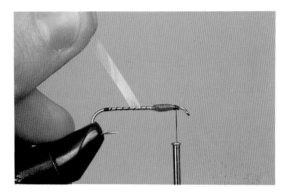

Continue winding until the right shape has been formed, then catch the loose end in at the eye.

Step 5

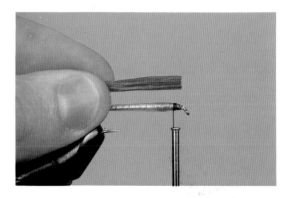

At this point you can varnish the body, which will add to the transparent effect. When dry, take a 2-inch length of brown or olive Raffene (plastic raffia). This will provide the dark countershaded back of the fish.

Step 6

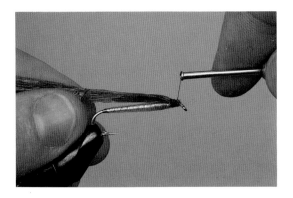

Wet the Raffene, which will help it to stretch, and catch it in at the eye. Tie off the thread and cut.

Step 7

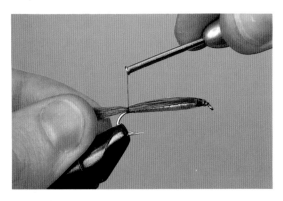

Catch the tying thread in at the end of the body, stretch the Raffene over the back and bind it down with turns of thread, finishing off with a five-turn whip finish.

Step 8

Allow to dry before adding an orange false hackle and finish off with coats of varnish to both head and tail whippings. Although it's not in the original pattern, you can add an eye to the head if you like.

Flat Metal Tinsel

Metal flats are the traditional method of creating bright, flashy bodies. Colours are somewhat limited, gold and silver being the main two, but they come in a wide variety of widths, which makes them useful for flies ranging from small winged wets to the superb fully-dressed salmon flies.

But metal tinsel does have one or two drawbacks. First, being very stiff and with sharp edges, it is not easy to tie in, though when used well it is exceedingly tough. Second, and probably more important, because it is metal it is prone to tarnishing, and it is not uncommon to return to a once-pristine sparkling salmon fly to find the body dulled and sadly lack-lustre. Still, metal tinsel does have its uses and if you are ever intending to tie the beautiful fully-dressed salmon flies it is a technique which must be acquired.

The tying sequence illustrates a popular salmon and sea-trout pattern, Kenny's Killer, which in this case is dressed on a size 4 loop-eyed salmon iron.

Step 1

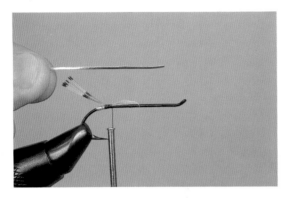

Run a length of black tying thread to the bend and form a tag from eight turns of fine round silver tinsel and a tail of golden pheasant tippet feather. Select 3 inches of wide oval silver tinsel.

Step 2

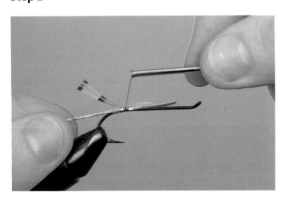

Catch the tinsel in at the bend so that the waste end lies along the total length of the hook shank, falling just short of the eye.

Step 3

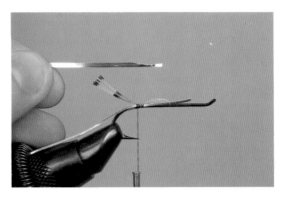

Remove 4 inches of wide flat silver tinsel from the bobbin. If it has tarnished already you will need to clean it first. This can be done with a standard metal polish, buffing to a shine with a cloth or strip of chamois leather. Prepare the tinsel for catching in by cutting a scallop-shaped indent close to the tip. This method is better than cutting to a point as it gives the thread something to bite on, preventing the tinsel from moving as winding begins.

Step 4

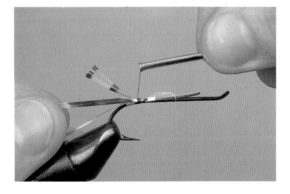

Catch in the tinsel at the tail, as shown in the drawing, and wind the thread back up to the eye in neat touching turns. It is essential that this foundation is as even as possible. If it is lumpy or uneven in any way it will be almost impossible to achieve the flat, even effect required of the tinsel body.

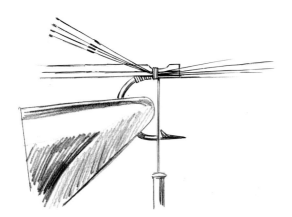

Step 5

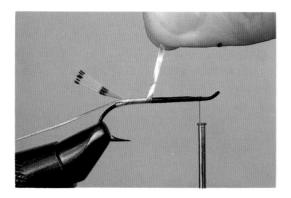

Begin to wind the tinsel. The first turn is the most difficult, but with the scalloped cut it shouldn't move and the tinsel should bend easily. If all is fine continue the tinsel up the hook shank.

Step 6

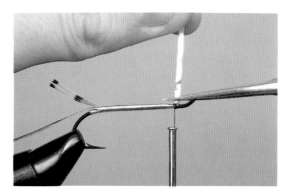

When a point just short of the eye is reached catch in the tinsel and trim off the excess. Be careful, though; metal tinsel is sharp and may cut the thread unless care is taken. The best way to prevent this is to make two or three turns without pulling them too tight, then the tighter binding turns may be taken over these buffer wraps.

Step 7

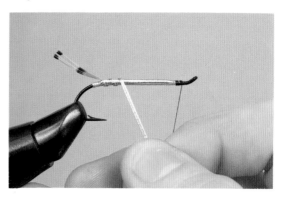

Finally, wind the oval tinsel up the body in a neat open spiral, in the opposite direction to that in which the flat tinsel was wound. This helps the ribbing to grip.

Step 8

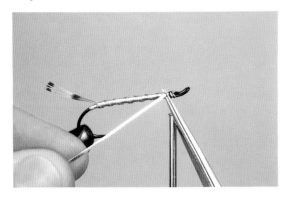

Catch the ribbing material in at the eye and trim off the excess.

Step 9

Complete the dressing with a wound swept hackle of dyed yellow cock hackle and a wing of black squirrel tail. The Kenny's Killer.

Lurex

Lurex and other similar materials such as Lureflash and Flashabou are metallised plastics, which combine the sparkle of the metal tinsel with the anti-tarnish property of the plastic. This makes them ideal for all types of bodies originally tied with metal tinsel, and, what's more, because these plastic tinsels are produced in a vast range of colours and effects they are far more adaptable than their predecessor. Indeed, being softer, many are mobile enough even to be used for winging, adding extra sparkle and a whole new avenue for experimentation.

The only drawback with Lurex is that it is not as robust as metal, and although it makes very good bodies, particularly when ribbed for strength, it should not be used for ribbing itself. Like metal tinsel, Lurex comes in a range of widths. Here a medium width is being used to form the body of a popular reservoir lure, the Goldie.

Step 1

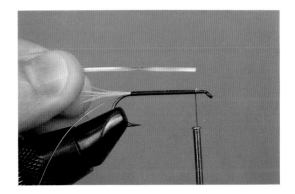

Run a length of black tying thread to the bend of a size 6 Partridge Bucktail/Streamer hook. There catch in a few fibres of dyed yellow cock hackle as a tail and 3 inches of gold wire. Take the thread back up the shank, remembering to form an even underbody. That done, cut 5 inches of medium-width gold Lurex from the bobbin.

Step 2

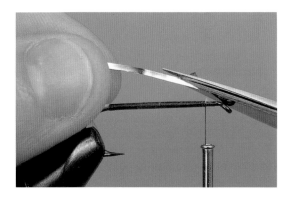

Cut one end to a point.

Step 3

This point helps start the winding process and prevents any unsightly bumps in the finished body.

Step 4

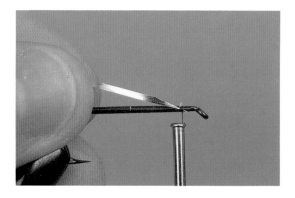

Catch in the Lurex by the point.

Step 5

Wind the Lurex down to the bend, making sure that each turn is even and butted up flush to the previous one.

Step 6

When you reach the tail take the Lurex back up to the point where it was caught in, secure the free end and remove the excess. This double wrap of Lurex helps produce a very even body.

Step 7

Complete the dressing by winding the wire rib before adding a false hackle of dyed yellow cock hackle fibres and a wing of yellow squirrel tail overlaid with a small bunch of black squirrel tail.

Mylar Piping

Because of its large diameter, Mylar piping is really applicable only for bigger lures and flies. Here, though, it excels; the wonderful metallic scale effect makes it perfect for small-fish imitations, or just when a great deal of body sparkle is needed. Originally the material was available only in plain gold and silver, but, since the huge increase in the types of metallic tinsels produced, shimmering greens, blues and pearls have given Mylar piping a whole new dimension.

Whatever type you use, the basic technique is the same. The piping comes in three diameters – small, medium and large – you choose the one which best suits the size of the hook and the depth of the body required. The pattern in the tying sequence is a simple Black and Gold Hairwing. The hook is a size 8 Partridge Bucktail/Streamer and the piping of medium diameter.

Step 1

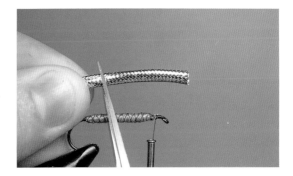

Because Mylar piping is a metallic tube formed round a removable central core, an underbody needs to be produced to give support to the finished body. The type of underbody depends upon the way the pattern is to be fished, and can be of lead, buoyant plastic foam or simply floss, which has a negligible effect on the fly's action. Here the latter is used, and it doesn't matter what colour it is as it will be completely covered. With the underbody formed, cut away a section of Mylar piping approximately one and a half times the length of the hook shank.

Step 2

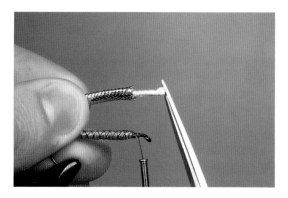

With a pair of tweezers or scissor tips remove the central core and discard it.

Step 3

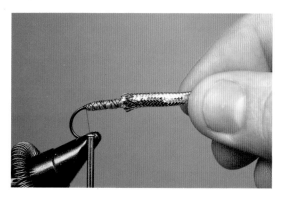

Take the tying thread down to the bend and gently slip the piping over the eye, sliding it down until it projects just past the underbody. Care must be taken in handling the piping at this time as it frays easily.

Step 4

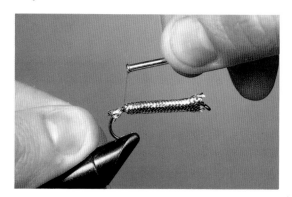

With the tying thread bind down the open end securely to the hook shank.

Step 5

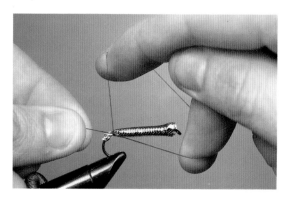

Tie off the thread at the bend with a five-turn whip finish.

Step 6

Carefully trim off the Mylar which projects past the tail whippings. As an alternative this may be left, though much longer than in the photograph, to form a sparkling tail.

Step 7

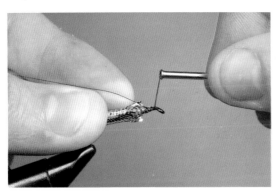

Run the tying thread back on at the eye.

Step 8

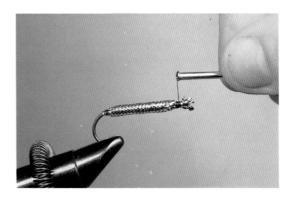

Next, pull the Mylar piping tight up towards the eye, catching it in place with turns of thread. As with the tail, trim off the excess before completing the pattern with a wing of black squirrel tail and a black beard hackle.

Step 9

Though the tail whippings may be left plain black, I prefer to add a tag of fluorescent red or orange floss. This should be formed and varnished before you begin the remainder of the dressing. The Black and Gold Hairwing.

Floss Silk

Although we traditionally speak of floss silk, by no means are all flosses made from natural silk. Many are produced from man-made substances, notably rayon, which has the advantage of spreading smooth whilst being wound but the disadvantage of being easily frayed. Still, with a little care this problem can be readily overcome.

The tying sequence illustrated below is based on the Royal Coachman, a very bright pattern, popular throughout Europe and the United States.

Step 1

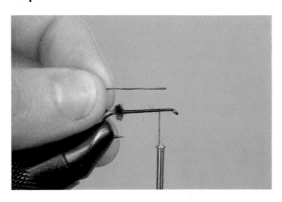

With black tying thread catch in a few fibres of golden pheasant tippet at the normal tail position of a size 12 Partridge nymph hook. Then, using a single strand of peacock herl, wind a full butt before carrying the thread for two-thirds of the way back up the shank. Next, take 4 inches of bright-red floss. If single-strand rayon is used that is fine, but if it is natural silk floss you will find that it comes as two strands twisted together. Used in this state it cannot produce a smooth body so the strands must be separated and used individually.

Step 2

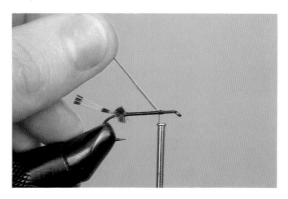

Catch the floss in by one end.

Step 3

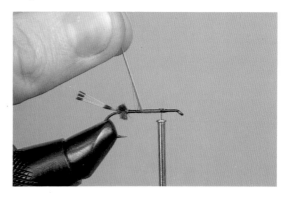

Begin to wind the floss down the hook shank.

Step 4

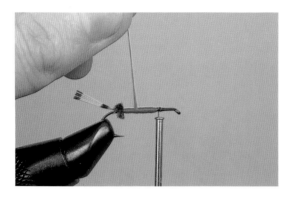

As you wind the floss the fibres will separate and flatten, producing a smooth effect. Continue until the butt has been reached before taking the floss back up to the point where it was first caught in. On smaller flies two layers will be enough, but on larger flies the layers can be built up until the correct bulk is produced.

Step 5

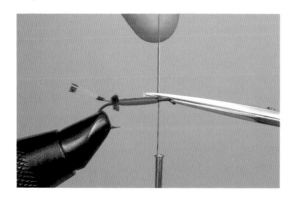

When the catching-in point is reached tie in the loose end and trim off the surplus.

Step 6

Complete the pattern with a brown cock hackle and a wing of paired slips of white duck quill. The Royal Coachman.

Peacock Quill

Peacock herl has already been dealt with in this chapter, but peacock feather may be used in another way. The herls in and just below the eye of a peacock feather have a central quill which is distinctly marked, giving a fine segmented appearance useful for producing the bodies of ephemerid and chironomid imitations.

Step 1

The first step is to prepare the quill. Basically, before it is tied in the quill must be stripped of the tiny iridescent herls which run its length. This may be achieved by various means – from ladies' hair remover and hot wax to manual stripping with a fingernail, a knife blade or an eraser. Whichever method is used care should be taken not to fracture the quill. In the illustration a rubber eraser is being used, stroked firmly but gently along the length of the quill.

Step 2

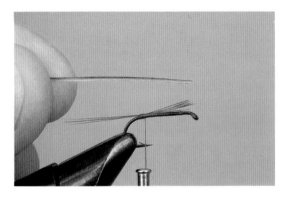

After preparing the quill, form the foundation for the pattern – in this instance the Ginger Quill – by running brown tying thread on to a size 14 Hooper dry-fly hook, and catching a few fibres of brown cock hackle in at the tail.

Step 3

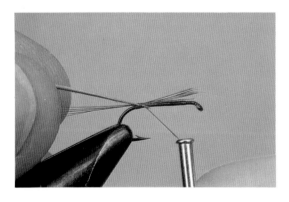

Catch the quill in at the tail and run the thread back up the hook shank. If a slightly fuller body is required, build up an even, tapered effect with turns of tying thread.

Step 4

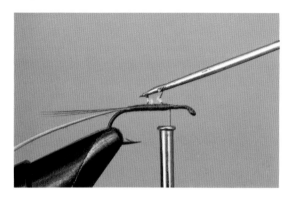

To give extra strength to the quill, a layer of varnish may be added to the body and allowed to dry to tacky before winding.

Step 5

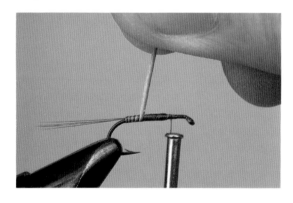

Take hold of the quill and wind it gently up the body in butted turns, making sure that there are no gaps.

Step 6

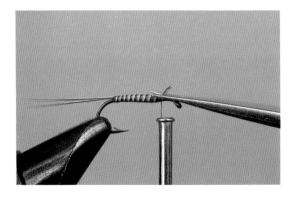

Catch in the loose end and trim off the waste.

Step 7

Complete the dry split-winged Ginger Quill by adding paired slip wings of grey duck and a good-quality ginger cock hackle. The Ginger Quill.

Hackle Bodies

As an extension to the technique of palmering (dealt with in detail in Chapter 8), it is possible to form a fly body completely from wound hackles. Obviously such a hackle-bodied fly is going to be very bushy indeed, accentuating the original properties of the pattern. For instance, bob flies tied this way will create a tremendous wake whilst dry flies become incredibly buoyant, perfect for use in very fast broken water.

Flies tied in this fashion, particularly if the hackle fibres are very long and air-resistant, also make ideal patterns for dapping – a technique where the line and fly catch the breeze and are blown out on the water's surface rather than being cast.

For the tying sequence I have chosen a dry fly, the Shadow Mayfly, a none too true-to-life dressing but nevertheless an effective one when trout are taking large mayfly duns.

Step 1

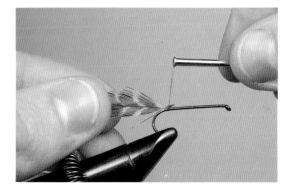

Fix a size 10 Captain Hamilton nymph hook in the vice and run a length of brown tying thread down to the bend. Choose a good-quality grizzle cock hackle; one with fibres approximately one and a half times the width of the hook gape is about right. Remove the base fluff and catch it at the bend by the bare stalk.

Step 2

Grasp the hackle tip with a pair of hackle pliers and begin winding it up the hook shank in neat touching turns.

Step 3

When the hackle has been fully wound, tie in the tip and remove the excess. That done, prepare another hackle of similar size and catch that in where the first hackle ends. I prefer to tie in the hackles one at a time rather than catching in a number all at the bend. My way, even if one hackle should break, the fly can still be used.

Step 4

Keep adding hackles until two-thirds of the hook shank have been covered and a 'flue brush' effect has been created.

Step 5

To complete the Shadow Mayfly, add wings of brown cock hackle tips and a collar hackle also of grizzle cock slightly longer in fibre than for the body.

Hackle-Point Bodies

Although a minor technique, some interesting flies may be tied with combined tails and body produced from a single cock hackle point. The method is most applicable to small and medium-size dry flies, particularly those where lightness is at a premium.

Step 1

After fixing a size 14 Hooper dry-fly hook in the vice, run a length of brown tying thread down to the bend. Next, select a blue dun cock hackle with fibres slightly longer than the hook shank.

Step 2

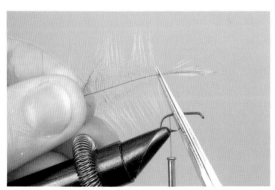

Holding the hackle by its tip, stroke back the fibres 'against the grain' so that they lie at right angles to the centre stalk. Then with a pair of scissors remove the tip.

Step 3

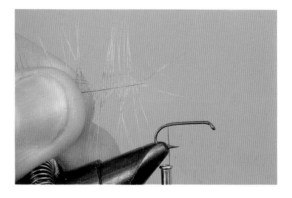

Stroke back into their original position two fibres on each side of the stalk. These will form the tail of the fly.

Step 4

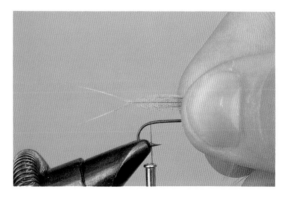

Change hands and stroke the remaining fibres back even further so that they lie right back along the stalk.

Step 5

With two loose turns of thread catch the hackle in at the bend a short way in front of the hackle tails.

Step 6

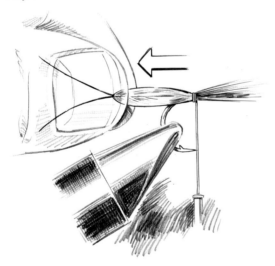

Gently grasp the tail and pull it through the turns of thread until the body projects back from the hook for the same length as the shank. Forming the body in this way will keep the body fibres even and tight. If they do come out of alignment, remove the hackle and start again. If all is OK, bind down the body securely, as shown in the photograph.

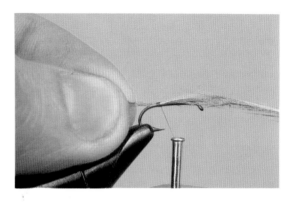

Step 7

Complete the dressing by adding a dubbed half body of mole fur plus a wound and divided hackle of blue dun cock, backed with brown feather fibre. The Hackle-Bodied Spinner.

Hackle Stalk

The use of hackle stalks as a body material has a long tradition. They provide a subtle segmented effect in a number of dry-fly patterns, especially those imitating the spent female spinners of various ephemerid species. The advantage of hackle stalk is that it is both tough and cheap, since you use up the large feathers at the back of a cape that so often go to waste. Hackle stalk also makes a good substitute for the more fragile stripped peacock quill. What's more, the natural taper and slight buoyancy of the hackle stalk give an even tapered result, which does nothing to detract from sparsely-dressed patterns intended to sit right in the surface film.

The pattern here is from a range designed by William Lunn, one-time river keeper on the Houghton Club beat of the River Test. The Lunn's Particular and two other patterns of his tying, the Yellow Boy and the Houghton Ruby, all imitate the spent spinners of various mayfly species and all have bodies of stripped hackle stalk of varying colours.

Step 1

Fix a size 14 dry-fly hook in the vice, run a length of fine crimson tying thread on just behind the eye and carry it on down to the bend. There catch in a few fibres of red game cock hackle as a tail.

Step 2

Select a large red game hackle from the back of the cape. Make sure the stalk is as long as possible before it begins to widen and become pithy towards the base.

Step 3

Carefully remove the fibres from the stalk, starting at the tip and working down to the base. Remove the still feathered tip then catch the bare stalk in at the hook bend by the point.

Step 4

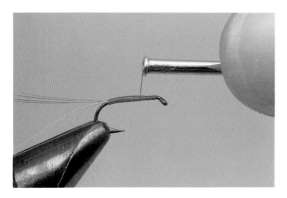

Take the thread three-quarters of the way back up the shank in neat touching turns. A neat underbody is essential as without it, winding an even body will be very difficult.

Step 5

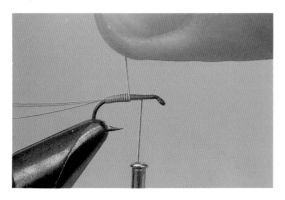

Take hold of the stalk and wind it up the hook shank, again in neat turns, each carefully butted up against the previous. If you find that the hackle stalk is too brittle and begins to break up under the tight turns (often a problem with the stiffer genetic hackles), it may be softened by soaking in water for a few hours. Obviously, if this is a problem it is a good idea to soak a good batch of stalks prior to a tying session.

Step 6

That done, complete the dressing with a pair of blue dun hackle points tied spent as wings and a few turns of medium-red game cock hackle. The Lunn's Particular.

Latex

Over the past decade, latex dental dam has been used to produce some visually superb imitations of many aquatic creatures, from caddis pupae to stonefly nymphs, from shrimps to crayfish. I use the term 'visually' because, although many latex dressings look absolutely fantastic, I trust fur and feather more to produce truly imitative patterns. This, though, is my opinion and one not held by all tyers, so I cannot discount the material completely. It certainly does look good, giving a lovely segmented appearance, which fits the imitative bill rather well. It can also be dyed a variety of colours, but I prefer to use the natural colour, marking it with a Pantone pen to suit the colour of the creature I am imitating.

One of the first dressings latex was put to was a caddis pupa imitation, and I am using one for the sequence.

Step 1

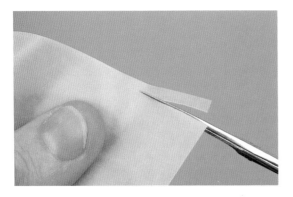

With a pair of sharp scissors cut a strip of latex 2 inches long by ³⁄₁₆ inch wide.

Step 2

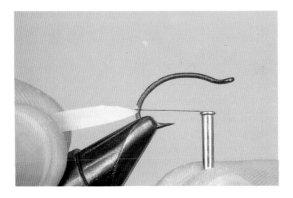

Prepare the hook, which in this case is a size 10 Yorkshire Sedge hook, by running on a length of brown tying thread down to the bend. Then cut the latex strip to a point and catch that in.

Step 3

To produce the required tapered maggot shape, an underbody has to be formed. Here pink Superla dubbing has been used, though floss or dubbing in various colours can be equally effective. If the colour is a very strong one, the translucence of the latex will allow it to show through, creating an interesting effect.

Step 4

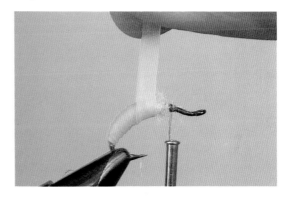

Putting slight tension on the latex strip, wind it over the underbody in even turns. Do not pull too tightly or the strip will become too thin and will also bed down unevenly. If one turn looks wrong simply undo it and try again. Do not relax the tension, though, or the whole thing will either slip or just unravel.

Step 5

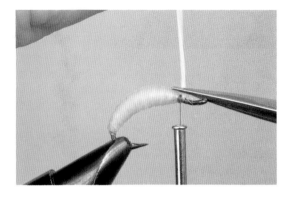

When you reach the end of the underbody and the body looks right, pull the latex tight to reduce its bulk and catch it in with tight turns of thread. Remove the excess as usual.

Step 6

The pattern may be completed with a thorax-cum-hackle of spun and clipped brown rabbit fur; this technique, though using squirrel hair, is shown at the end of Chapter 7. The Latex Caddis Pupa.

Monofilament

Though I am not a lover of plastics, particularly in imitative patterns, nylon mono does produce a very interesting segmented effect applicable to a number of larval and pupal dressings. One is Carnill's Buzzer, a chironomid midge pupa imitation which, by sheer coincidence, is the pattern used here.

Step 1

Fix a size 12 Yorkshire Sedge hook in the vice and run on black tying thread, taking it well round the bend to help give the hooked buzzer profile. There catch in a small tuft of white marabou. Cut off 3 inches of Black Streak, a prestretched nylon monofilament with a D cross-section.

Step 2

Cut one end of the nylon into a sharp point and catch it in at the same spot as the marabou.

Step 3

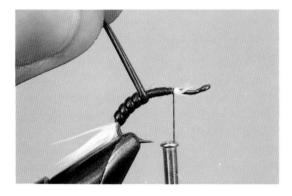

Take the tying thread two-thirds of the way back to the eye, then, keeping the nylon taut, wind it in closely-butted turns to where the thread stops.

Step 4

Tie the mono in and cut away the waste. The dressing is completed with a plume of marabou for the breathing filaments and a thorax of dubbed mole's fur backed with a slip of black goose herl. An optional extra comes in the form of wing buds, produced by trimming to shape fibres taken from the waste side of a white goose primary feather. A final step is to trim short the marabou filaments at both head and tail. The Carnill Buzzer.

Deer-Hair Heads

For many years now the buoyant property of deer body hair has been used to provide natural floatability in a vast array of dressings. From tiny hopper patterns to imitations as varied as upwinged flies and even small bait fish, all have benefitted by the incorporation of deer hair in their tying.

Though the uses of deer hair are varied, it is as the spun head of the Muddler range that it is known to most fly fishers. The original Muddler Minnow, invented by Don Gapen, has spawned an enormous number of patterns. Some, like the original, mimic small fish, whilst others suggest anything from a grasshopper to an adult caddis skittering across the water's surface. Many imitate nothing, being merely stimulators of the fishes' natural aggression or curiosity. What they all have in common is a head of spun deer hair. This head, which may be as fine or as large and densely packed as the tyer requires, creates a wonderful turbulent action, either when 'waked' across the surface or when retrieved deep on a sinking line. It is an action which has resulted in the downfall of countless game fish world-wide.

As a Muddler is a style of tying rather than an individual pattern, most dressings may be adapted as the tyer requires. Whatever the pattern, the procedure illustrated in the following sequence remains the same. In this case the dressing is for a Hen Hackle Muddler. Dressed on a Partridge Bucktail/Streamer hook, this fly may be tied in a range of sizes to suggest a wide variety of creepy-crawlies.

Step 1

As the deer hair is added as a head, the body and wing of the fly should be produced first. In this case the dressing consists of a tail of paired brown hen hackle tips, a body of dubbed hare's fur, a wing again of paired brown hen hackle tips but overlaid with strips of wood duck, and a hackle of speckled brown hen hackle, long in the fibre. The important point, which is the same for all Muddler-headed patterns, is that the dressing should stop well short of the eye, leaving the remaining one-third of the hook shank bare, ready to accept the spun hair. That done, take a piece of deer hair on the skin and remove a small bunch of hair along with the brown speckled tips.

Step 2

Don't use too much hair at once. The amount illustrated is quite adequate. Ensure that the tips are even, and then offer the bunch up to the hook so that the tips project back half-way along the shank.

Step 3

Change hands and hold the bunch in place parallel to the shank.

Step 4

Take one loose turn of thread over the hair close to the base of the wing. Don't pull tight yet.

Step 5

Take another two loose turns over the deer hair, slowly pulling tight. This will cause the hair to spin round the hook shank and flare as the thread bites. This would be a fault in tying a wing, but in tying a Muddler head it is just the result you are trying to achieve.

Step 6

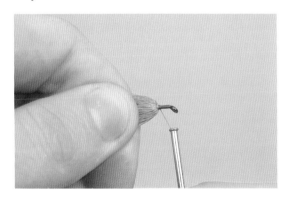

Pull the butts of the hair back and take three or four tight turns of thread round the hook shank to secure the bunch firmly in place.

Step 7

You are now ready to add further bunches, building up the head. Keep repeating this process until the whole of the bare shank has been covered. The number of bunches obviously depends on the size of the hook – the smaller it is, the fewer bunches required.

Step 8

Use fingers and thumb to tamp back the hair clear of the eye. This has the effect of compacting the hair as well as exposing the eye ready for the whip finish.

Step 9

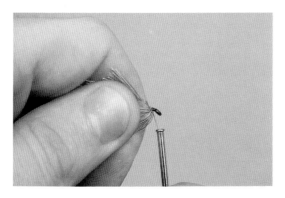

When you are sure that you have added as much hair as you need, make three or four turns behind the eye and complete with a whip finish.

Step 10

What you now have in the vice should resemble a rather untidy bottle brush. All that needs to be done is to clip it to shape with a sharp pair of scissors.

Step 11

The scissors used for trimming away excess hair may have either curved or straight tips. My preference is for the latter. Either way, the best method is to give the hair a rough trim, removing the bulk, before following up with a second, more precise cut. The finished shape depends much on the style in which the pattern is to be fished. For surface lures the head may be left large to create as much fish-attracting wake as possible, whilst for subsurface patterns the head should be trimmed tight to sink more easily.

Step 12

Profile, too, may vary – from round and bulbous to teardrop or bullet, as shown in the illustration. The larger and more water-resistant the head, the more buoyant it will be. Finally, complete the dressing by allowing a few drops of lacquer to soak along from the eye into the base of the hair and thread. This will prevent the head from twisting during use and make it more robust.

Deer-Hair Bodies

As a development of the standard Muddler head, deer hair may also be used as a complete body to create some very killing patterns where a buoyant but soft effect is required. Fry and snail imitations, which need to sit right in the surface film, are obvious examples. Bass bugs, too, improve greatly when deer hair is used instead of other materials such as hollow plastic or cork. The problem with solid incompressible bodies is that the fish are able to get hold of them without taking the hook properly, resulting in many abortive takes. The softness of deer hair produces a more natural fly, which is taken more positively and gives a far better proportion of hook-ups.

One of my favourite uses for deer hair is in buoyant fry patterns. In this instance it is an imitation of a perch fry, but deer hair can be used to imitate any small bait fish, such as roach, chub or minnows. When this style of dressing is used the pattern is invariably fished either 'dead drift' or retrieved slowly around weed beds, suggesting a small fish in its final death throes as a result of disease or a previous attack by a predator.

Step 1

Fix a size 4 JS Streamer hook in the vice and run on a length of black tying thread. Catch in, just short of the eye, a pair of bead chain eyes painted black (the technique is described in Chapter 9). Behind them bind in two tufts of dyed red cock

hackle fibres, one either side of the hook shank, as pectoral fins. Then run the tying thread down to the bend in tight touching turns. Form the tail by winding on two or three turns of dyed red cock hackle, pulling the fibres back and then trimming to length with a pair of scissors. Leaving the thread at the bend, remove a bunch of bleached white deer hair from the skin and offer it up to the hook.

Step 2

Holding the bunch right at the bend, take two loose turns of thread over it. Make sure that the thread comes half-way along the bunch so when it flares both ends are roughly equal.

Step 3

Pull the thread tight so that the hair spins fully round the shank then give a few tight turns on the shank to secure it. From that point on simply keep adding further bunches of hair until the shank is covered from bend to eye. Remember not to use too large a bunch each time and make sure that each bunch flares completely around the shank to form an even ruff.

Step 4

The most tricky part comes when working the hair around the hackles and bead eyes. Take care to ensure that the hair doesn't get caught under the beads but flares properly to cover in the gap between the eyes. Keep pushing each bunch back to keep the hair compact.

Step 5

Finish off the actual tying with the mandatory whip finish. What you will be left with in the vice looks an absolute mess now but after a few minutes with a pair of scissors the transformation will be dramatic.

Step 6

Begin to trim away the hair, starting at the head. Work carefully round the pectoral fins, then down the sides of the body towards the tail. Gradually remove hair to produce a tapered fish shape. In the case of the perch fry, a fringe of hair should be left along the back to imitate the dorsal fin.

Step 7

The basic perch outline, trimmed to shape.

Step 8

Using waterproof Pantone pens, add colour to the hair to match the natural perch. Green and brown are the basic colours, with a little yellow along the belly, the remainder being left white to produce countershading. Three black stripes should be added to each flank to mimic those of the natural. If other more silvery fish are being imitated, little or no colouring should be used. Otherwise, stick to the colour scheme of the genuine article.

Complete the Deer Hair Perch Fry by adding a yellow eye with a black pupil.

Extended Deer-Hair Bodies

Although the traditional way of using deer hair is to spin and clip it, as illustrated in the previous two sequences, on smaller, finer patterns the bulk of the spun body is inappropriate, Even so, deer hair and its natural buoyancy may still be used to great effect either laid along the hook shank and bound down or, as here, to create detached bodies for mayfly dressings. Indeed, any dry pattern where a light extended body is required, such as the daddy-long-legs, will benefit greatly from this technique.

The following sequence illustrates the steps used for tying the body for a Thorax Dun, imitating the sub-imago of the larger, darker mayflies.

Step 1

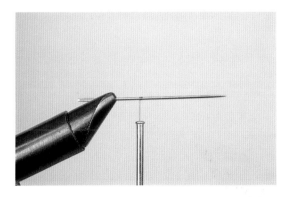

As the body is not dressed directly on the hook, a base is needed. An ordinary fine darning needle is perfect for the job and this should be fixed into the vice by the eye. Run on a few turns of brown tying thread and remove the waste end.

Step 2

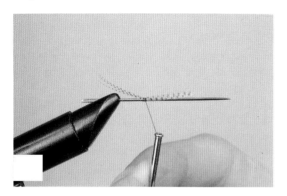

As this is to be the body of a mayfly, the next step is to catch in three fibres of speckled wood duck, to imitate the setae of the natural. Obviously, when imitating insects without tails these should be omitted.

Step 3

From a piece of deer body hair remove a small bunch. The illustration shows the amount required to produce a body compatible with a size 12 hook. If the fly you are tying is larger or smaller the amount will need to be altered.

Step 4

Holding the bunch by its butts, ensure that all the tips are even and then catch them in with three turns of thread directly over the position at which the tails were caught in. Make sure the tips project forwards up the needle for as short a distance as possible. The hair will naturally flare but this is perfectly all right.

Step 5

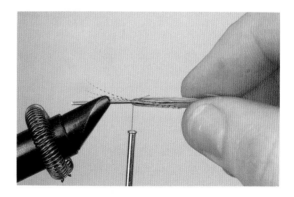

Pull all the hair butts back up the needle towards the point. As you do so, allow the thread to pass through the hair so that it remains in the position in which it was left. The other point to remember is to ensure that all the hair is pulled evenly so that no loose loops or lumps are formed.

Step 6

Wind the thread up toward the needle point in a neat open spiral. Don't pull too tight, though, as this will cause the thread to bite in, ruining the effect. As each turn is made ease the hair back straight so that the pull of the thread doesn't cause it to twist.

Step 7

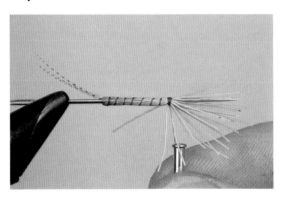

Once you have created enough body, finish off with half a dozen good tight turns and a whip finish. The length of body depends on the size of fly being tied, but as a rule it is always better to produce too much body and then trim it to length as it is tied to the hook.

Step 8

The final step is to gently ease the body along and off the point of the needle. A few drops of lacquer may then be soaked into the hair to make it more robust. Once dry, the body should be caught in at the bend of a dry-fly hook. In this case it is a size 12 Partridge barbless down-eye. The fly is completed with a wing, again of deer body hair, plus a parachute hackle of soft blue dun cock and a thorax of brown Antron. The Deer Hair Thorax Dun.

Woven Chenille

To most inquisitive 'thinking' angler-entomologists it quickly becomes apparent that, although the body of an insect can be described in a single colour – usually olive, brown, black, and so on – closer inspection reveals that the colour is made up of a subtle mixture of hues. Instead of a 'solid' olive-green, a combination of greens, yellows and browns produces the overall effect. To this end, as fly tyers we produce a wide range of material blends to make a more lifelike imitation. Often, too, an insect, particularly the larva, is countershaded, the back being darker and better camouflaged than the belly. Here, though, a different technique is needed, one which allows materials to be worked but will create both a mottled and countershaded result. This is where weaving comes in.

Many stranded materials can be woven to

produce some very interesting effects, from raffia and wool to floss silk and chenille. Floss and chenille are perhaps the most popular. Obviously, the finer the material the longer it takes to produce the effect, so floss is better suited to smaller nymph patterns, such as imitations of ephemerid larvae. For larger dressings, such as stonefly and dragonfly nymphs, chenille makes a superb alternative, giving a wonderfully succulent effect whilst having the added advantage of being quick to tie.

The illustrated sequence is the tying of a dragonfly nymph – to be specific, the nymph of the Libellulid, or darter dragonfly. The tying is by one of the United States' top fly dressers, Darrel Martin.

Step 1

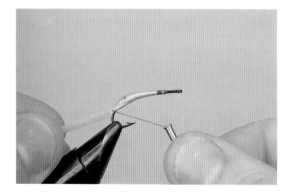

The hook in this case is a size 8 Partridge K12ST. After fixing it in the vice, run a length of brown tying thread on at the eye. Build a neat layer of touching turns of thread before catching a length of floss silk a quarter of the way back down the shank. In order to make the abdomen the oval shape of the natural, a corresponding underbody should be built up using the floss. Because it is to be covered in chenille, colour is unimportant. That done, remove the herl from the end of a length of chenille and catch it in at the bend.

Step 2

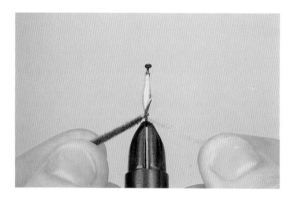

Catch in a second length of chenille at the same point. In order to create the required countershading it should be of a darker shade than the first, or even a completely different colour. In this example I have used two shades of green, though the choice is yours and depends much on the creature being imitated. I have also used sueded rather than standard chenille, as it is tougher and is less likely to break up whilst being worked.

Step 3

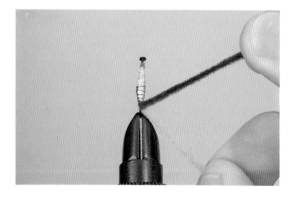

Take both strands of chenille and pull them over to the right-hand side of the hook.

Step 4

Keeping both lengths taut, pull the lighter-coloured strand up and over the darker.

Step 5

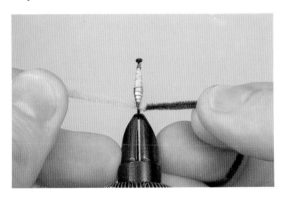

Next pull the lighter strand under the hook shank so that one strand is on each side of the shank.

Step 6

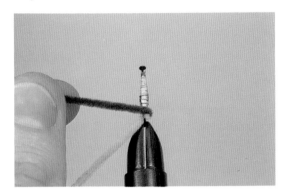

Next pull the darker strand over the back of the shank, so that both strands are on the same side.

Step 7

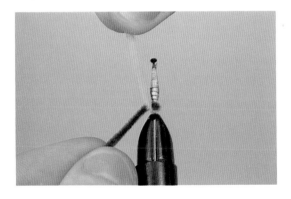

Now pull the lighter strand up over the darker, and towards the hook eye.

Step 8

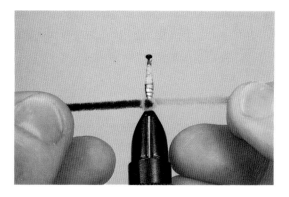

Then take it under the shank to the opposite side. Keeping the ends taut, take the darker strand over the back of the shank to the same side. You will now be back at Step 3 but with a single woven sequence complete.

Step 9

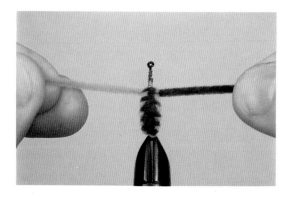

Repeat this sequence, working up the shank towards the eye until the whole of the underbody has been covered. Remember to keep the order of the colours as stated. If you don't the effect will be reversed, with a light back and dark belly. If you do lose your way, simply go back to Step 3.

Step 10

To complete the dressing of the Woven Dragonfly Nymph, add a pair of black painted lead eyes, wing cases of olive feather fibre, legs also of olive feather fibre knotted once, and a thorax and head of olive marabou dubbed on. As an optional extra, antennae of two wood duck fibres may be added just in front of the eyes.

Plaited Marabou

Although a minor technique, when a very light body with plenty of movement is required there is little to beat an extended body of plaited marabou. It is best suited to tyings fished slowly just subsurface, particularly where they would normally be tied on a large hook, with the subsequent weight problem. A good example of this is damselfly nymph imitations.

When these large, spindly nymphs are ready to emerge as adults they can be seen swimming with a deliberate lashing of the abdomen, making for marginal vegetation, up which they climb prior to emergence. Here the plaited marabou body makes an ideal alternative to the normal rigid, inanimate longshank hook.

The only drawback to this technique is the susceptibility of the marabou to damage during fishing. Little can be done to prevent this and the only consolation is that when the fish are proving very difficult the light, lifelike action of plaited marabou can make all the difference.

Step 1

As the aim is to produce an extended body, free of the hook, a base is required on which to plait the marabou. A fine darning needle fits the bill admirably. Run on a length of olive tying thread just behind the point, then tear off a bunch of long olive-dyed marabou fibres.

Step 2

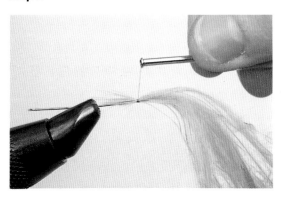

Ensuring that the tips of the marabou are all even, catch in the bunch with three turns of thread.

Step 3

Allow the tips to extend back for approximately ½ inch. These will imitate the tails of the natural. Finish off with a whip finish, allowing a very tiny drop of lacquer to soak into the bare threads. You are now ready to plait the marabou.

Step 4

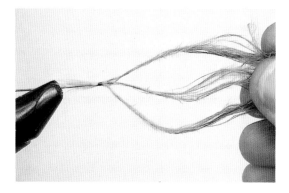

Divide the marabou into three equal strands. If the fibres keep springing apart they may be dampened slightly to give better control.

Step 5

The actual plaiting may look difficult but is really quite simple. Keeping a slight tension on the strands, pass the top strand through the gap beween middle and bottom. Next, pass the bottom strand through the gap between the middle and the original top strand (which was pulled down to the bottom during the first plait). Now pass what was the middle strand (but is now the top) through the gap between the remaining two, pulling the bottom strand to the top. All three strands should now be back in their original order but with one plait made. With the strands in front of you, the technique is simpler than it sounds in print. The drawing should help.

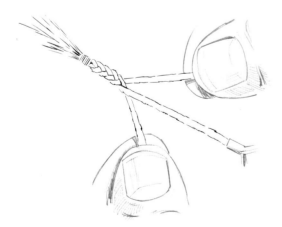

Step 6

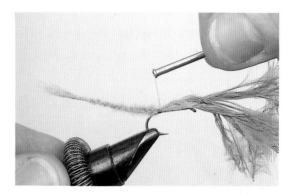

Repeat the process, building up approximately ¾ inch of plait. The natural taper of the marabou will give the body its required profile. That done, remove the marabou from the needle and catch in the plait by the butt at the bend of a size 12 Captain Hamilton.

Step 7

To complete the dressing, add a thorax of dubbed marabou the same colour as the body, legs of brown partridge tufts and wing cases of olive feather fibre. As the eyes need to be as light as possible, each may be formed by putting a single overhand knot into a length of suede chenille, as shown in the drawing. The Plaited Marabou Damselfly Nymph.

Make a single overhand knot in the sueded chenille before drawing tight.

The translucency of the dubbed body gives sparkle and life to any pattern.

6 Ribbing

Ribbing is an integral part of forming the body of a fly and it is worthwhile concentrating on a few of its finer aspects. The purpose of ribbing is threefold: to imitate, to adorn, and to protect. The distinction between the three properties is a little clouded – and in many dressings either two or all three of them overlap – but they do serve as a guide to which type of rib to use.

From the point of imitation, the ribbing suggests the segmentation and body markings of the natural creature. This property is most prevalent in nymph and dry-fly patterns where the aim, if not purely imitative, is at least towards suggesting a small living creature, be it a shrimp, caddis, or aquatic insect. But a rib can also provide more than just a static jointed effect. Movement, too, may be introduced with the addition of materials such as ostrich or peacock herl, which have long fibres and work admirably, imitating the gill filaments running along the body of many aquatic nymphs. Adornment, on the other hand, is where a rib is used merely to introduce shine or sparkle. Many streamers and hairwings use either metal or non-tarnish plastic tinsels and Mylars to create that extra little attraction; these often gaudy patterns imitate little, living or dead, and catch fish which take the fly out of aggression or sheer curiosity. The only fly in the ointment, if you will forgive the pun, comes with patterns designed to imitate small bait fish. Here the flash of a metallic rib mimics that of the fry.

The third, protective, purpose of ribbing is to help hold the body together and preserve it from damage during fishing. Many delicate materials require a good solid rib to prevent them being destroyed during the rigours of casting or under the sharp attention of a fish's teeth. Feather fibre, such as marabou and goose herl, is prone to damage and even if the herl is wound over a layer of wet varnish the extra strength of a rib is well worthwhile.

Once you have decided whether a body should or should not be ribbed, what ribbing material do you use? Here a second consideration comes in – how the finished fly is intended to be fished. For instance, a slip of olive goose herl makes an ideal body both for nymph and adult ephemerid patterns, but which of the two it is to be used for does make a difference to the ribbing material.

Traditionally, ribs were almost always made from some type of metal, be it oval braid, flat plate or fine wire. This may be all right for patterns, such as nymph imitations, which require the sparkle that the metal gives as well as the extra weight. Conversely, a dry fly, which obviously is intended to float, requires no additional weight, and in the case of dun imitations no extra sparkle, the naturals being uncompromisingly matt. Here materials such as stripped hackle stalk, which is itself slightly buoyant, and monofilament nylon, which is very strong and light, make excellent alternatives.

Hackle Stalk

Hackle stalk is indeed a great material for ribbing the bodies of small dry flies, and because the stripped stems of the large hackles at the back of a cape are ideal, feathers which would otherwise go to waste are made use of. Here in the dressing of a small Golden Olive Midge dry fly the hackle stalk gives segmentation to the body whilst adding negligible weight.

Step 1

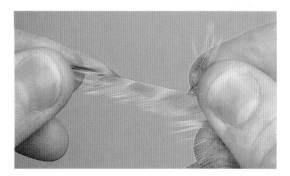

Select any large cock hackle and strip away all the fibres from it.

Step 2

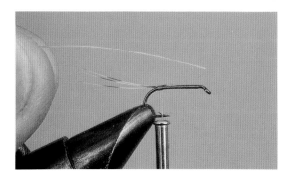

After fixing the hook in the vice, in this case a size 14 Captain Hamilton Dry Fly, run on a length of brown tying thread. At the bend catch in a few fibres of grizzle cock hackle to form the tails, then offer up the stripped hackle stalk, point first.

Step 3

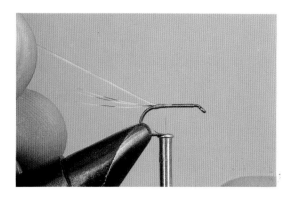

Catch in the hackle stalk by its tip then dub on the thread a pinch of rabbit underfur dyed golden olive.

Step 4

Wind the dubbed fur up the shank to a point just short of the eye. Take hold of the hackle stalk and begin to wind that, too, up the hook over the body in the opposite spiral. This will prevent it bedding too deeply into the fur.

Step 5

Catch in the butt of the hackle stalk just behind the eye and trim away the excess. Complete the dressing by adding two turns of grizzle cock hackle as a collar. The Golden Olive Midge.

Monofilament Nylon

In my opinion nylon monfilament is all too little used as a ribbing material. I can't understand why, though, for it has many plus points. Not least is its lightness-to-strength ratio, so that even monofilament as fine as 1/140 inch with a breaking strain of 5lb is far stronger than most metal-based tinsels, as well as being abrasion-resistant. The fact that nylon monofil is available in a wide range of thicknesses and colours – from black and brown through light green to clear – means that it can be put to an even larger range of tasks. From tiny dries to large nymphs, to provide both translucency and strength, nylon has much to recommend it.

Used in conjunction with a much more fragile material, nylon monofil allows yet another effect to be produced. The other material in the example is ostrich herl – a fine, filamentous product, well able to suggest the abdominal gills of various nymphs, in this case a mayfly nymph.

Step 1

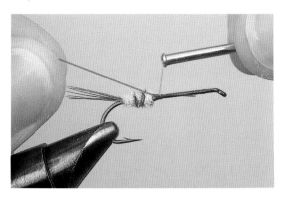

The hook is a size 10 Captain Hamilton Nymph hook. Run on a length of brown tying thread down to the bend. There catch in six fibres of cock pheasant tail. Dub on a short section of buff hare underfur and rib it for two turns with the butts of the pheasant tail. This suggests the abdominal markings of the natural. Next catch in 3 inches of brown monofil of approximately six-pound breaking strain.

Step 2

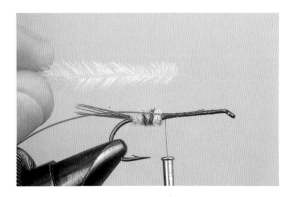

Remove a strand of buff ostrich herl and prepare it for catching in. This is achieved by stripping the herl from 1/4 inch at the base of the strand.

Step 3

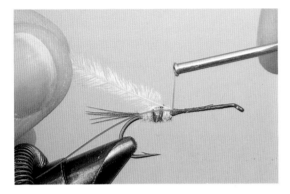

Catch in the strand by the stripped section. Next, dub on more hare fur and wind it up the shank for two-thirds of its length. This forms the abdomen.

Step 4

Take hold of the ostrich herl and wind it up over the body in a neat open spiral. Four or five turns will be sufficient on a hook of this size. Because the fibres at the base of the strand are the shortest, the fibres get longer as they are wound up the body, giving an even, tapered effect.

Step 5

Secure the waste end of ostrich herl then take hold of the nylon monofil. That, too, should be wound up towards the eye in a neat open spiral. Exactly the same number of turns should be made, but in the opposite direction. If you wound the herl in a clockwise direction (looking from the hook eye) the monofil should be wound anticlockwise. This ensures that each turn of monofil crosses and locks each turn of herl rather than just lying by its side. This is the key to an effective rib.

Step 6

The dressing is then completed with a thorax of dubbed hare fur and wingcases and legs of cock pheasant centre tail, tied in the same way as for the Walker Mayfly Nymph described Chapter 5. The Mayfly Nymph – with gills of ostrich herl.

Flat Metal Ribbing

The next technique uses a rib to give sparkle and life, suggesting the gas trapped within the cuticle of an aquatic insect close to the point of emergence. The Gold Ribbed Hare's Ear nymph – or GRHE nymph for short – is a wonderful pattern, not truly imitative but suggestive of all types of aquatic nymphs, a point which probably makes it all the more effective. Not only is it a killing pattern but it has the further merit of being very cheap and easy to dress, consisting of merely a hook, brown tying thread, a pinch or two of hare body fur (*not* hare's ear – body fur is longer in the fibre and better) and a short length of flat gold tinsel.

Step 1

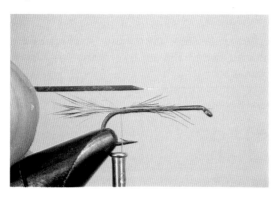

Once the hook, a size 12 Captain Hamilton nymph hook, is in the vice, run brown tying thread down to the bend and catch in a few brown hare guard hairs. Take a 2-inch length of flat gold tinsel and cut one end to a fine point. Although metal tinsel does tarnish, it is used here rather than Lurex purely because it is stronger.

Step 2

Catch the tinsel in by the point.

Step 3

After dubbing on a body of brown hare fur, take hold of the gold tinsel and wind it up over the body in an open spiral. Four turns should be enough. Unlike the nylon monofil and ostrich herl combination, this rib can be wound in either direction, depending on what you wish to achieve. If it is wound in the same direction as the hare fur it will bed down and become less obvious, giving more of an inner sparkle. In the illustration it is wound in the opposite direction, which makes it more obvious.

Step 4

Before forming the thorax, tie off the tinsel. Make the final turn of the tinsel *on top* of the preceding one and hold it taut while you bind it down with several turns of thread. Cut away the waste.

Step 5

Complete the dressing by adding a thorax, again of dubbed hare's fur. That done, with the tip of a dubbing needle gently pick out the fibres both in the thorax and from under the rib to give the 'buggy' appearance which is so much the hall-mark of this pattern. The Gold Ribbed Hare's Ear nymph.

Clear Plastic Ribbing

Clear or translucent plastics make ideal ribbing materials for a vast range of nymph patterns. From proprietary brands such as Swannundaze to simple clear polythene strip, all give an extra sparkle to imitative dressings, suggesting the gas trapped within the nymphal skin, so much the mark of nymphs on the point of emergence. Some, like clear polythene, actually trap a little air under the dressing, which further enhances the effect.

The trapped gas gives some creatures a 'coating' of silver over the base colour of the adult's body beneath. The chironomid pupa at the point of hatching is a very good example of this and one of my own dressings, the True-to-Life Midge Pupa, mimics this. As a result, it fishes well wherever the natural is to be found.

The pattern may be dressed on a range of sizes to cover at least the large- to medium-size species. Here the tying is on a size 12 Captain Hamilton.

Step 1

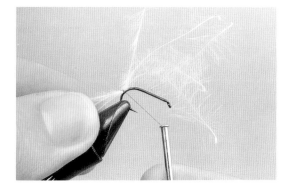

After fixing the hook in the vice run a length of brown tying thread to a point well round the bend. You may find it easier if the hook is angled slightly downwards in the vice, at least for this first stage of tying. This mimics the curved profile of the natural. There catch in a small tuft of white marabou.

Step 2

From a piece of clear polythene cut a strip twice the width of the intended rib, in the same way as for the Polystickle described in Chapter 5. In this case it should be ⅛ inch wide. That done, gently stretch the polythene. This will halve its width to ¹/₁₆ inch and also make it clearer. Cut one end to a point and catch it in at the same point as the marabou.

Step 3

At the same point, catch in a slip of black goose herl and a slip of dyed red goose herl, the latter half the width of the former. Adjust the hook in the vice to a normal position, take the thread two-thirds of the way back to the eye, and follow it with the black goose herl.

Step 4

Wind the red herl over the black in an open spiral. Then take hold of the polythene strip and wind it over the herl in the opposite spiral. Although the aim is to almost cover the herl, small gaps should be left allowing the herl to poke through.

Step 5

Complete the dressing by adding vestigial wings of brown goose biot clipped to shape, a thorax of dubbed rabbit underfur, a shell back of grey feather fibre and breathing filaments, protruding over the eye, of white marabou. The True-to-Life Midge Pupa.

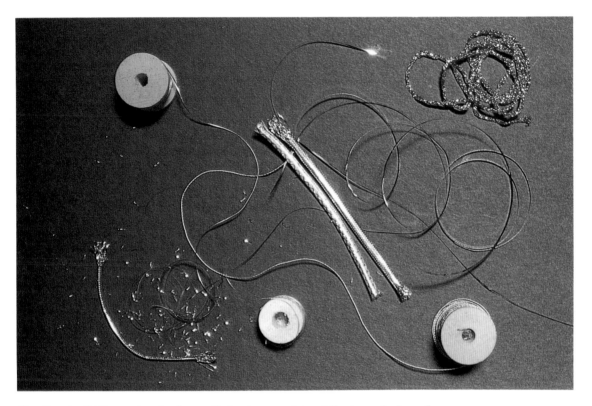

The glint of a rib lifts any dressing from a diminutive nymph to a fully-dressed salmon fly.

7 Hackles and Legs

The hackle of a fly can cover a multitude of sins. It can suggest the flickering legs of the nymph, or the buzz of legs and wings as a newly-hatched dun floats off downstream; it can even suggest the fins and tail of a small fish. More generally it can be used to give structure and life to our artificials.

With such a diverse subject there are many styles, from the simple collar to palmered, body, beard and parachute hackles, in an even greater range of materials. This chapter covers the major techniques plus a few which are less commonly used but offer great potential.

Simple Dry-Fly Hackles

This collar style is the standard method for hackling most dry flies, both of traditional and modern dressing. It is simplicity itself, the main prerequisite being a supply of top-quality cock hackles in a range of colours. Unfortunately this isn't as easy as it sounds, for although the technique itself is quite straightforward, obtaining the correct hackles is not. It appears to be a matter of supply – there are just not enough high-grade capes being produced to meet the growing demand.

To bridge the gap left by the normal free-range supply of capes from India and China, birds are now being reared purely for their hackles. These are no ordinary farmyard fowl, though, but are bred specially for their incredibly high-quality feathers. The two best-known producers are Metz and Henry Hoffman, and between them they have shown us hackles of a quality previously unheard of – capes containing literally hundreds of feathers just right for tying all the standard-size dries, right down to the tiniest no-see-um. My only slight reservation with this type of hackle is the thickness of the stalk. For some reason, particularly in the natural reds, the centre stem of the genetic hackle is much thicker than its wild counterpart and there doesn't appear to be a great deal of difference between the grades. This can cause a few problems when it comes to winding neatly, but can be countered if special care is taken to keep each turn of hackle perfectly butted up against the previous one.

Unfortunately this superb quality doesn't come cheap, and the genetically-produced hackles are initially very expensive, a single grade 1 cape costing over £50. That said, if you are serious about tying top-quality hackled dries, this type of cape is certainly worth considering.

For the illustrated sequence of tying a simple dry-fly hackle, I have chosen a simple dry fly – the Red Tag. This is a lovely little pattern dear to the hearts of many autumn grayling anglers. Dressed in this case on a size 14 Captain Hamilton fine-wire dry-fly hook, the red wool tail and peacock herl body have already been formed.

Step 1

After tying in the body, select a natural red cock hackle of the correct size. If you bend the hackle into a curve you will be able to examine the fibres more easily. They should be approximately twice the length of the hook gape.

Step 2

Making sure that there is enough room between the body and eye to accept the hackle, trim its end to shape, removing all base fibres and leaving a slightly serrated effect which will help the thread to grip.

Step 3

Catch in the prepared tip with three tight turns of thread.

Step 4

Taking hold of the hackle tip with the hackle pliers, begin to wind towards the eye. Ensure that the hackle goes on with the shiny side to the front. Occasionally you will get a hackle which refuses to wind without twisting over. If this happens, remove it and prepare another.

Step 5

Once you have completed three or four turns to give the correct density to the hackle, carefully wind the thread through the hackle to give extra strength, catch in the loose tip and trim off the surplus. Finally, stroke the fibres back clear of the eye before building a small, neat head and giving a whip finish.

Step 6

After removing any fibres which have been trapped at the eye, give two coats of varnish to the bare threads. The Red Tag.

Simple Wet-Fly Hackles

Although the techniques used for tying both dry- and wet-fly collar hackles are very similar, there are a few specific differences. Most obvious is the type of hackle used. Where that of the dry fly is designed to keep the fly afloat, the wet-fly hackle should have a more streamlined profile, allowing easy entry into the water. Also, the fibres should be softer to work well in the current and impart all-important movement and life.

Here the softer hen hackles come into their own; the more absorbent webby fibres are soon soaked and help the fly to sink. With the move towards more sparsely-hackled patterns, tyings such as the Greenwell Spider are finding increasing favour.

Step 1

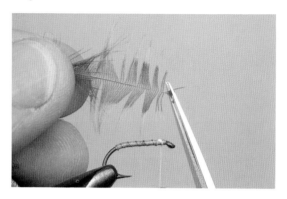

After fixing a size 14 or 16 down-eyed wet-fly hook in the vice, form a standard Greenwell body from waxed primrose Gossamer silk, ribbed with fine gold wire. Waxing the tying thread in this way gives it a delicate olive hue. That done, select a light furnace hen hackle and, after stroking back all the fibres so that they lie at right angles to the stalk, remove the tip with a pair of scissors.

Step 2

Catch the hackle point in at the eye.

Step 3

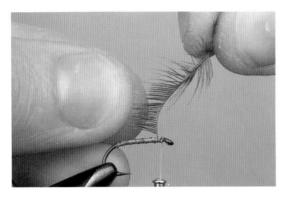

At this stage you can either wind the hackle as normal or 'double' it, a technique whereby the fibres of the hackle are drawn back so that both sides lie together, which doubles their density and causes the fibres to lie at a shallower angle to the hook shank. This is accomplished by holding the hackle taut and drawing the fibres back repeatedly between finger and thumb until they stay in place, as in the drawing.

Step 4

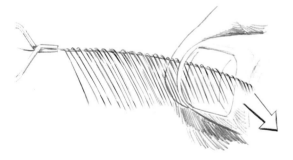

The doubled hackle. As an aside, this method is also used for preparing the body and throat hackles for fully-dressed salmon flies.

Step 5

Take hold of the hackle butt and wind on two full turns. It pays in this style of dressing to keep the hackle sparse.

Step 6

Secure with three turns of thread and trim off the surplus.

Step 7

The Greenwell Spider.

Wound and Swept Hackles

The traditional method for hackling most winged wet flies is with a wound cock or hen hackle swept back and held in position with turns of thread to conform to the standard throat-hackle configuration. In essence it is very similar to the simple wet-fly hackle.

Step 1

After preparing the body – which in this case is for a size 12 Fiery Brown – choose a soft-fibred natural red cock or hen hackle. Select a hackle with fibres slightly longer than the gape of the hook.

Step 2

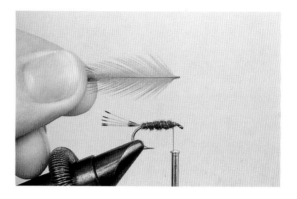

Trim away the base fluff so a small section of stalk remains, with the fibres cut to produce a serrated effect.

Step 3

Catch in the hackle butt with two turns of thread.

Step 4

With a pair of hackle pliers wind on three or four turns.

Step 5

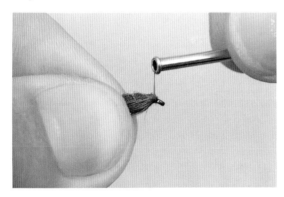

Catch in the tip and remove the excess. Then, between finger and thumb, stroke the fibres back away from the eye and below the hook shank. Once the fibres are in position bind them in place with turns of thread. The drawing shows the correct position in greater detail.

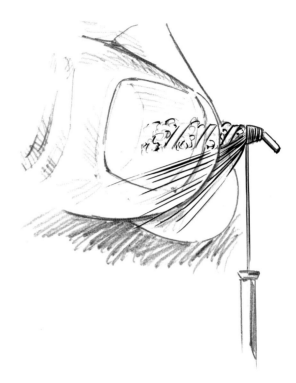

Step 6

Ideally, all the hackle fibres should lie to the sides and below the hook shank. Any that don't, and which might interfere with the tying in of the wing, may be removed with a pair of scissors.

Step 7

Complete the dressing by adding a wing of bronze mallard flank feather, finishing off the fly in the usual way. The Fiery Brown.

False Hackles

Though many fly tyers prefer the previous method for throat-hackling their wet flies and streamers, there is another method, if not quite as good then almost – the false hackle. The false, or beard hackle as it is otherwise known, is a very good method for using materials which either can't be wound in the normal fashion or are so long in the fibre that they would look out of proportion. Guinea-fowl, blue jay, various gamebird feathers and even hair may be pressed into service. In this vein it is also a good way of using up over-large cock hackles which would usually go to waste.

The pattern used in the illustrated sequence has a strong, albeit erroneous, Irish flavour to it, for although bright green and named the Leprechaun it is more at home on the reservoirs and lakes of southern England.

Step 1

To prepare the body of the Leprechaun, fix a size 8 or 10 Partridge Bucktail/Streamer hook in the vice and with black tying thread tie in a tail of bright-green cock hackle fibres and a body of fluorescent green chenille or seal fur, ribbed with oval silver tinsel.

Step 2

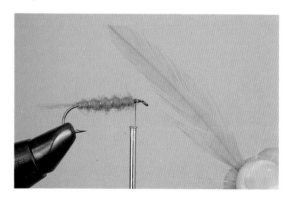

Select a large, bright-green cock hackle, long in the fibre.

Step 3

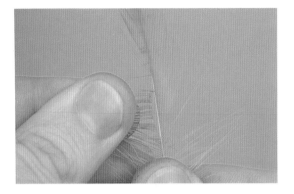

From the stalk tear off a generous bunch of fibres.

Step 4

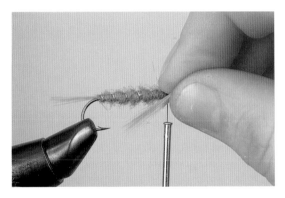

Offer the bunch up to the shank and judge for length. Ideally, the fibres should fall just short of the hook point.

Step 5

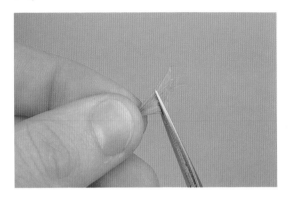

If the bunch is too long, trim it to length with a pair of scissors. Now is the time to get it right as it is very difficult to trim away the excess butts once the bunch has been tied in.

Step 6

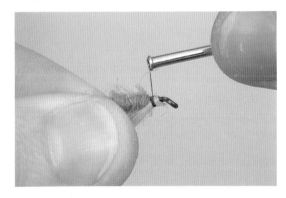

Offer the hackle fibres back up to the hook and, positioning them on the under side of the hook shank, wind two loose turns of thread over the butts.

Step 7

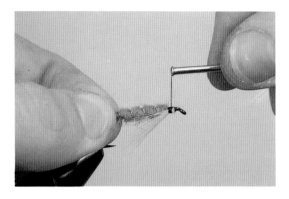

As you draw the thread tight, the natural side-ward pull of the thread will cause the hackle fibres to flare around the underside of the hook, as shown in the drawing.

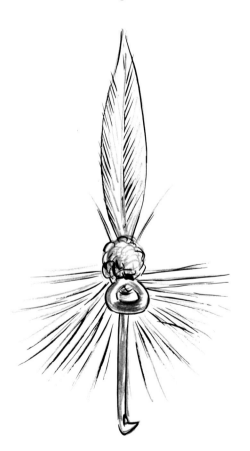

Step 8

Correctly applied, the false hackle can impart nearly as much movement as the wound and swept-back version. To complete the Leprechaun add a streamer wing of two pairs of bright-green cock hackles placed back to back. The Leprechaun.

Parachute Hackles

Whilst most types of hackle are wound around the hook shank in some way, there are varieties which break with this tradition. The best-known is the parachute style of hackling, in which the hackle is actually wound around a small projection from the top of the hook. This means that the buoyancy of the fly is above rather than below the body, ensuring that the body sits right in or just below the surface film. This in turn makes the style perfect for hackling spent and emerger patterns, though many traditional dressings may also be adapted to the parachute method.

Various ways have been devised to produce parachute hackles, from small metal projections forged with the hook itself to the addition of wire or hackle-stalk loops. I prefer the latter. Extra metal has little place in a fly that is designed to float, and if tied correctly the hackle-stalk loop is perfectly strong enough.

The pattern in the tying sequence is a variation of the Grey Duster, the Grizzle Duster, and is dressed on a size 14 Hooper dry-fly hook.

Step 1

After fixing the hook in the vice tie in three fibres of grizzle hackle as a tail and dub on a little blue rabbit underfur, winding it half-way up the shank. That done, select a grizzle cock hackle with fibres approximately one and a half times the length of the hook gape.

Step 2

Strip off all the soft and damaged fibres from the base of the hackle, leaving the bare stalk. Catch the hackle in by its base with two turns of thread but do not remove the bare stalk as normal.

Step 3

Instead, form a loop with the stalk, catching the end in again with turns of thread. This semi-rigid loop will act as the base upon which the hackle is wound.

Step 4

Take hold of the hackle tip and wind on one or two turns. The drawing shows this in detail. The beauty of the parachute hackle is that because all the hackle fibres come into contact with the water, fewer turns are needed to provide the necessary floatability.

Make two or three turns of hackle around the base of the stalk loop.

Step 5

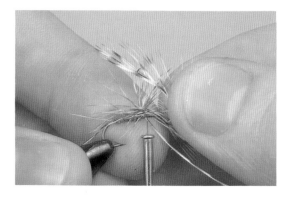

Once the turns have been made, push the hackle tip through the loop made in the stalk.

Step 6

Keeping hold of the tip, begin to pull both it and the stalk so that the loop traps the hackle tip in place.

Step 7

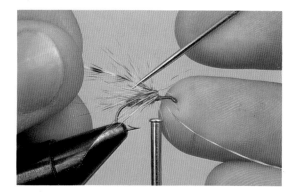

A few hackle fibres may become trapped. If so, simply tease them out gently with the point of a dubbing needle.

Step 8

Next, stroke all the hackle fibres back and at the same time pull the hackle tip forwards, securing it with turns of thread. If you leave the security of the hackle to the tension of the stalk loop alone the tying will not be nearly so robust.

Step 9

Remove the waste ends of both hackle tip and stalk, and then complete the front half of the body with dubbed rabbit underfur before finishing off the head in the usual way. Gently adjust the hackle fibres back into the parachute configuration so that they radiate evenly from the central stalk loop. A touch of varnish to the loop will further strengthen the hackle.

Step 10

The Grey Duster variant – parachute style.

Soft Hackles

The body feathers of a number of gamebirds are used as wet-fly hackles, noticeably in many North Country dressings. Grouse, snipe, partridge, both grey and brown, are all used. The method of tying is very similar to that for the simple wet-fly hackle. These soft feathers are very mobile and work well in the turbulent rough streams of their origin.

The pattern I have chosen for the photographic sequence is the Partridge and Orange, the body of which in this case is of orange floss ribbed with gold wire on a size 14 Captain Hamilton medium-weight hook.

Step 1

With the prepared body already in the vice, select a suitable brown partridge feather. Choose one which is well marked and as short in the fibre as possible.

Step 2

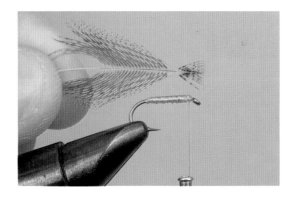

Stroke the fibres back to reveal the tip, which can then be trimmed to leave a short stub.

Step 3

Catch the stub in just behind the eye. Although cock and hen hackles can be caught in by tip or butt with equal ease, with soft body hackles it usually pays to use the tip. The stalk of such feathers is so thick towards the butt that it makes winding all but impossible.

Step 4

Make only one or two turns of hackle before catching in the butt and trimming away the excess.

Step 5

The Partridge and Orange.

Multiple Collar Hackles

This method of hackling is most applicable to dry flies, particularly those which need to be buoyant to ride a heavy riffle. It involves winding two or more different-coloured hackles through one another. The result is very pleasing to both trout and tyer alike, giving a beautifully mottled and very effective appearance.

One such pattern is the Grey Fox variant, which can be dressed on a size 12 down to an 18 but is always overhackled. The tail is simply a few fibres of natural red gamecock hackle and the body stripped hackle stalk applied to half the hook shank only, leaving plenty of room for the hackle.

Step 1

Once the body has been completed, select three good-quality cock hackles, one light ginger, one Plymouth rock and finally one of dark ginger.

Step 2

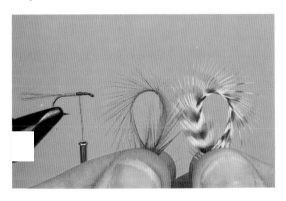

Judge all the hackles to make sure that they have fibres of approximately the same length, which should be at least two and a half or three times that of the hook gape.

Step 3

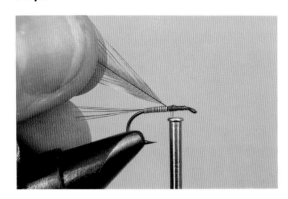

Strip the base fluff from each hackle and catch them in one by one at the very point where the body ends.

Step 4

The hackles in position.

Step 5

Take hold of the dark-ginger hackle and wind it towards but not too close to the eye.

Step 6

The winding sequence in this case is dark ginger, Plymouth rock and finally light ginger.

Step 7

Once the hackles have been wound and the tips secured, remove them before building a small neat head.

Step 8

The Grey Fox variant.

Palmered Hackles

The palmered or body hackle is equally applicable for both wet and dry flies. In the wet the extra hackle gives added movement whilst in the dry buoyancy is much improved, though at the cost of a denser outline. The technique can even be applied to salmon flies, where the hackle may also be doubled prior to winding.

The palmer style of fly has always been popular with the loch fisher, the dense, bushy hackling making superb top dropper flies, perfect for holding on the wave. Though hen hackles can be used, I prefer soft cock hackles, which have that extra spring to them, helping to create the seductive and all-important subsurface wake.

Of the patterns which fall into this category, one of my particular favourites is the Wickham's Fancy. Not only does it work exceptionally well on stillwaters but when tied as a dry fly it is a very good river pattern around sedge time. Although it may be tied with wings of grey duck primary, in this instance I have gone for the wingless version.

Step 1

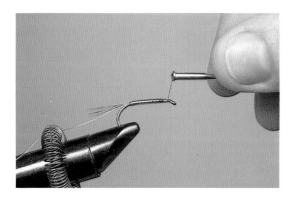

Fix in the vice a size 10 Partridge Sproat and run a length of brown tying thread down to the bend. There catch in a few fibres of red game hackle as a tail and 3 inches of gold wire or fine round tinsel. Complete this first stage with a body of gold Lurex, leaving the thread a short distance from the eye.

Step 2

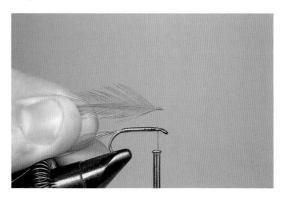

Select a soft, 'webby' light-red cock hackle, trimming away the fluffy base fibres to leave a short stub.

Step 3

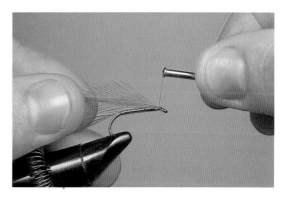

At a point slightly further from the eye than for a standard collar hackle, catch in the stub.

Step 4

Take hold of the hackle tip with a pair of hackle pliers and begin to wind it down the hook shank towards the tail. Keep the spiral open and even, approximately five turns being enough.

Step 5

When you reach the tail, maintain tension on the hackle while you wind the gold rib through it, up towards the eye. This secures the hackle stem to the body.

Step 6

Catch in the ribbing at the eye and trim off the surplus ribbing and hackle point.

Step 7

Complete the fly by adding a few turns of extra red game hackle in normal collar style before building a small neat head.

Hair

Hair is not usually thought of as being a suitable material for hackling a fly. True, the technique required is not particularly easy and does take a little time to master. Like all good things, though, it is well worth the effort.

Many types of hair may be used, including rabbit dyed a variety of colours, and squirrel. I am very fond of the latter, as not only do the hairs have a beautiful mottling but I can use up the soft base of the squirrel tail which so often goes to waste. Hair hackles are more than the name would suggest as the soft underfur of the animal as well as the stiffer, longer guard hairs is used. This produces a combined hackle and thorax and as such is a method well suited to nymph and bug patterns. Stonefly nymph and caddis pupa imitations are two good examples.

In the illustrations I have used an Amber Caddis Pupa dressed on a Yorkshire Sedge hook. As the hair hackle involves only the front third of the hook, the abdomen has already been tied (*see* Chapter 5).

Step 1

Complete the abdomen of your pattern, leaving the third of the hook nearest the eye free, ready for the thorax and hackle. Form a loop 2 or 3 inches long in the tying thread.

Step 2

From the hair you are going to use (in this case the base of a natural brown squirrel tail) remove a small tuft containing both guard hairs and softer underfur.

Step 3

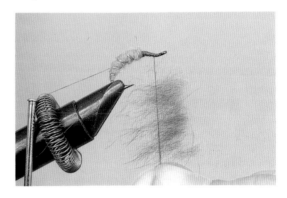

Remove any extra-long guard hairs so that all the tips are even and place the prepared tuft within the loop of thread. Spread the hairs out thinly along the length of the loop.

Step 4

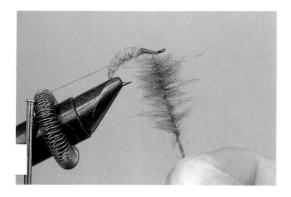

Twist the loop so that all the fibres are trapped firmly and spin out like a bottle brush. Plenty of twists are needed to produce the desired effect.

Step 5

Simply wind the hackle over the hook, working towards the eye. The soft underfur will provide the bulk whilst the longer guard hairs will simulate the legs and antennae. Catch in the end of the loop and trim off. With dampened finger and thumb, work the fibres gently so that they lie back along the hook. If there is too much bulk trim off some of the hair on the top and sides of the thorax.

Step 6

The completed Hair Hackle Caddis Pupa.

Legs

Although in most flies the suggestion of legs comes from the 'buzz' effect of the hackles, this isn't always so. There are a variety of imitations, usually of terrestrial insects, that make great play of the creatures' legs. Included in this category are dressings for grasshoppers of various kinds, as well as hawthorn and heather flies, both terrestrial members of the order Diptera. Perhaps the most famous, though, is the cranefly or daddy-long-legs, a large, weak-flying, gangling creature which hatches off in large numbers during the autumn months. Its long trailing legs are well catered for in all daddy imitations.

The dressing I have used for the illustrated sequence is a standard stillwater pattern dressed on a longshank size 8 Captain Hamilton nymph hook.

Step 1

After placing the hook in the vice run on a length of brown tying thread down to the bend. The abdomen is formed by light-brown goose herl ribbed with nylon monofilament, the wings are a pair of light-grizzle hackle points. The all-important legs are produced by knotting cock pheasant centre tail fibres.

Step 2

Each fibre should be knotted twice with a simple overhand knot. These knots put a kink in the fibre and imitate the joints of the natural's leg. Take care when pulling the knots tight – too quick and hard and the fibre will break.

Step 3

Produce eight legs in all, dividing them into two bunches of four. For those quick to point out that as an insect the daddy should only have six legs, the answer is simple. As the legs are quite fragile extra ones are tied in to extend the effective life of this time-consuming dressing. In any case, the fish seem unable to tell the difference.

Step 4

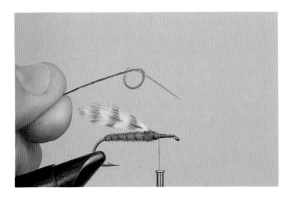

Catch in a bunch of four fibres on either side of the body, then trim off the excess butts.

Step 5

Build a thorax from the same brown goose herl as was used for the body.

Step 6

Complete the dressing with a few turns of light-grizzle cock hackle as a collar and a whip finish. The Daddy-Long-Legs.

Rubber Legs

As legs are first and foremost a means of locomotion, it seems fitting that the final sequence in this chapter should be dedicated to using legs to give a pattern incredible fish-catching life. Rubber strands are becoming ever more popular for imparting action to a whole range of flies, from buoyant bass bugs to nymphs and lures, and whilst I am not a fan of modern plastic materials in fly dressing, this technique, which produces a superb wiggly action when the fly is pulled through the water, is certainly of major interest.

The original pattern incorporating this funny-looking material was known as the Girdle Bug, a black-bodied dressing with six legs and two tails. The elastic material used for the legs was and is available from haberdashery shops for supporting various types of underwear, hence 'Girdle', I suppose. Today the elastic is sold by most suppliers of fly-dressing material.

As it is the kicking action of the legs that is the important factor, most rubber-legged flies are pretty simple, having bodies of either chenille or wool in a variety of colours. The pattern illustrated is equally simple but the body is of dubbed black rabbit fur. A whole variety of patterns may be given the rubber-leg treatment, some of which, such as the Montana Nymph, may be adapted from Chapter 5.

Step 1

The first step is to remove three strands from an elastic strip. These strips are preformed so the strands tear off easily and come in various thicknesses. The thinner the strand, the greater the action.

Step 2

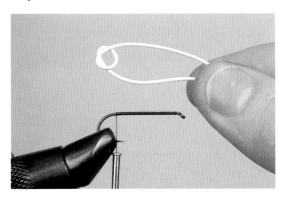

Fix a size 8 Captain Hamilton nymph hook in the vice and run black tying thread down to the bend. Then take a 2-inch rubber strand and make a single overhand knot half-way along its length.

Step 3

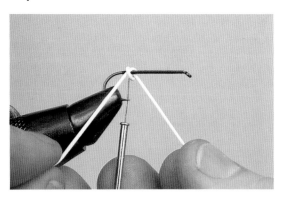

Slip the knot over the eye of the hook down to a point just short of the bend before pulling it tight.

Step 4

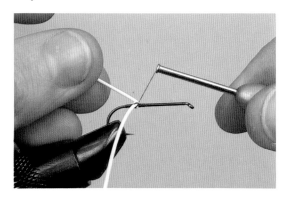

Bind the legs in position with figure-of-eight turns of tying thread.

Step 5

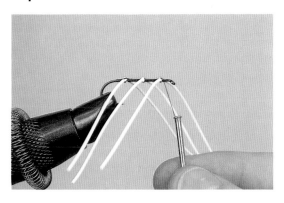

That done, take the thread one-third of the way back up the shank and repeat the process, then repeat again so that the three lengths, and the six legs, are attached.

Step 6

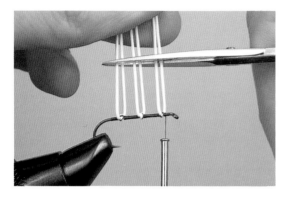

Trim the legs to the desired length. This is up to the individual tyer's requirements, for the longer the legs the greater the action in the water. Here, though, the legs are approximately the same length as the hook shank. To ensure that when they are trimmed all the legs are the same length, the strands should be drawn up parallel above the hook shank and cut in a single motion with a sharp pair of scissors.

Step 7

To finish, add a tail of fluorescent yellow Flashabou and a body of black rabbit fur dubbed on. The Rubber-Legged Rabbit.

From the subtle hues of the natural cape to the enamelled brilliance of the jungle cock.

8 Wings

Depending on the type of fly in which it is tied, the purpose of the wing is twofold. In the case of direct imitations, be they fished wet or dry, it is to copy the outline and structure of a specific natural creature, whilst in lures and streamers it is to impart movement and life. In the latter, materials are chosen which offer the greatest mobility, soft hair and marabou being prime examples.

There are times, though, when the two objectives overlap. Traditional wet flies and fry imitations are opposite ends of the same spectrum. Whilst some traditional wet flies are pure attractors, many are good suggestions of aquatic insects at the very point of emergence. Here the wing, slim and projecting low over the hook shank, imitates the blossoming wings of the natural and at the same time works with the hackle to give the pattern the desired life. With fry patterns, obviously small fish don't have wings, but hair or feather when pulled through the current forms a neat and convincing fishy outline, and some materials – notably marabou and the light, stranded plastic tinsels – pulse attractively with every twitch of the retrieve.

The techniques required for tying neat, robust wings are not difficult to learn, so it is all the more surprising that many fly dressers encounter real problems.

Hair Wings – Salmon

As a winging material, hair has much to recommend it. It is very robust, comes in a wide array of types and lengths, and it is also cheap and readily obtainable. Add to this the fact that it is available in any colour required and you can see why some fly dressers use hair, in its many forms, to the exclusion of all other materials.

Among the most popular types are bucktail, goat, calf tail, and squirrel, both in grey and various shades of brown. The technique of bleaching and dying grey squirrel tails has added a whole new dimension to this material. Where once only a dingy mottled effect was possible, squirrel tails now come in an array of bright sparkling colours, ideal for virtually all sizes of fly. Because of this I tend to use squirrel tail wherever possible. It is a fine, crisp hair which works well on both still and running water.

For small- to medium-size salmon flies it is ideal, particularly during summer conditions. For this reason I have chosen the hairwing adaptation of a traditional salmon pattern for the illustrated steps. The original Blue Charm has a wing of bronze mallard overlaid with barred teal flank. In this version both have been replaced by brown squirrel, with negligible loss of effect and a great increase in durability and ease of tying.

Step 1

To prepare the wing, take a brown squirrel tail and with the finger and thumb of the left hand draw a small bunch of the hair back from the central bone until the tips are even. Then, with a pair of scissors, remove the bunch so that the grey roots are included.

Step 2

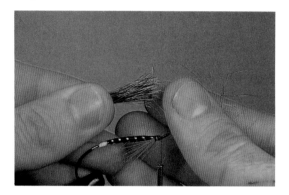

Remove the short, damaged and soft hairs from the base.

Step 3

Judge the bunch for length by offering it up to the hook shank. Trim the butts so that when tied in, the wing reaches the bend of the hook or slightly beyond it.

Step 4

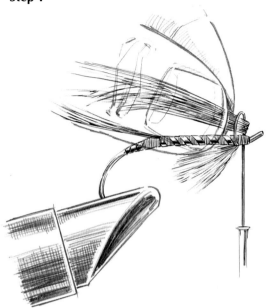

After trimming, offer the wing up to the hook so that the butts are exactly flush with the eye. Throw one loose turn of thread over the butts in a winging loop, making a downward pull with the thread to hold the wing in position.

Step 5

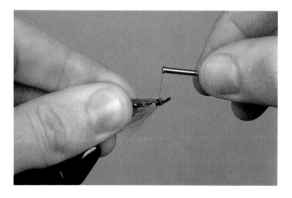

If the wing is aligned to your satisfaction, make a further five or six turns to hold the bunch in place.

Step 6

As an extra precaution, before finishing off the head run a little lacquer into the threads and allow it to soak into the hair butts. Hair is relatively incompressible, making it difficult for the thread to grip. This additional step will prevent the wing coming away during repeated casting.

Step 7

The hairwing Blue Charm.

The Hair Minnow

An extension of the simple hair wing is the hair-minnow style of tying. An American innovation, it makes superb fry imitations, being very robust and also exhibiting the required light belly, dark back countershading of the natural small fish.

Once you get the hang of the technique it is very simple and quick to produce.

Step 1

Fix a longshank hook in the vice and run on a length of tying thread, carrying it only one-third of the way down the hook shank. Although a tinsel body can be added I prefer simply to use a silvered hook. And while red tying thread is usually advocated I prefer to use black for the majority of steps, finally adding a collar of fluorescent red floss. From a white bucktail remove a bunch of hair. Ensuring that all the tips are even, tease out all the damaged fibres and fluff. Offer it up to the hook to judge for length.

Step 2

Reverse the bunch of hair and catch it in under the hook shank so that the points project past the eye approximately one and half times the length of the hook.

Step 3

Trim off the excess hair.

Step 4

Next, repeat the process with a bunch of brown bucktail of similar size, but this time catch the bunch in on the top of the shank.

Step 5

Draw the white bucktail back under the shank and tie it back with four or five tight turns of thread.

Step 6

Do the same with the brown bucktail, securing with a five-turn whip finish.

Step 7

Finally add a collar of fluorescent floss before soaking the head with three or four coats of varnish. This makes the fly extremely robust.

Step 8

As an addition, the sides of the head can each be given an eye (*see* Chapter 10). The Hair Minnow.

Hair Wings – Dry Fly

Along with its durability, the inherent buoyancy of some types of hair makes it ideal as a winging material for dry flies. Deer hair and bucktail are two of the most widely used, the latter being incorporated in the Wulff series – probably the best known of all the hairwing dry flies. The dressing in this case is for the Grey Wulff.

Step 1

From the base of a plain brown bucktail remove a substantial bunch with a pair of scissors. The actual amount depends on the size of hook being dressed and can only be judged on that basis. From the butts remove all the fluff and damaged fibres.

Step 2

Ensure that all the tips are even (*see* the drawing on page 43) and offer the bunch up to the hook so that it projects over the eye a distance approximately two-thirds the length of the hook shank. Bind it down with three tight turns of thread.

Step 3

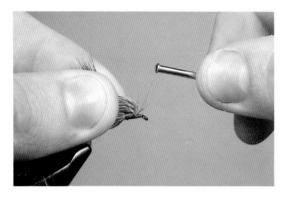

Once you are satisfied with the length, throw six or seven turns of thread in front of the wing just behind the eye. This will make the wing lift.

Step 4

Carry the thread down the body over the butts and run a small amount of lacquer into the base of the wing.

Step 5

Using scissors, trim the waste butts so that they taper towards the tail. This will help to produce an even effect when the body is formed.

Step 6

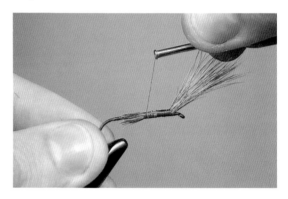

Continue winding the thread over the butts, bringing it back up to the wing. Although not the prescribed method, I often leave the wing as a single bunch, particularly in smaller patterns.

Step 7

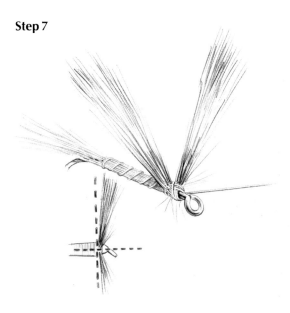

If you require the traditional Wulff-style V wing, on reaching the wing divide the bunch into two equal parts, separating them with figure-of-eight turns of thread wound through the butts.

Step 8

The dressing may now be completed by adding a tail of bucktail, a body of rabbit underfur and a blue dun cock hackle. The Grey Wulff.

Paired Feather-Slip Wings

The traditional and still widely-used method for winging wet trout flies incorporates two matched slips of quill feather placed back to back. They are intended to represent the wings of various species of Ephemeroptera and the effectiveness of the method can be measured in time if nothing else. Originally many types of feather were used – blackbird, moorhen, even water rail – but latterly, due much to conservation measures and a sensible attitude by fly tyers, these have been replaced by various types of duck feather. The ubiquitous mallard is now the main source of suitable feathers; in fact, if anything, the quills are better than the feathers they replace, being strongly webbed and very robust as well as coming in just the right shades of smoky grey.

Step 1

The first step is to choose the right feathers for the job. These should be primary feathers selected from opposite sides of a pair of duck wings. Make sure that you pick corresponding quills so that they are as alike as possible, with the same degree of curve. Doing so will make tying a neat wing much easier.

Step 2

From each quill remove slips of equal width. Use the tips of a pair of scissors to separate the fibres before removing each slip. Various tools are available to do this job, but after a little practice you will find the scissor points just as good and more practical. Exact width is very much personal preference but I like such a wing on hooks from size 10 to 14 to contain from ten to twelve fibres on each side.

Step 3

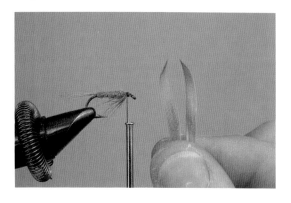

Before presenting the wing to the fly body, judge the slips for size, holding them so they curve together dull sides in. In this instance the pattern is a Blue Dun tied on a size 14 Captain Hamilton, and from the illustration you can see the position and space left between body and eye ready for the wing.

Step 4

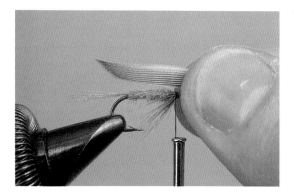

When you're satisfied that they are identical, place the two slips together so that the tips are even and the natural curves of the slips cancel each other out, producing an absolutely straight wing. Hold the wing over the body to judge for length; ideally it should be approximately one and a half times the length of the hook shank.

Step 5

Grasp the wing between finger and thumb, holding it in position, and throw a single loose turn of thread over the butts.

Step 6

With the bobbin holder directly below the hook shank, give a steady downward pull. This 'winging loop', as it is known, prevents the wing being drawn out of position by the normal sideways winding action of the tying thread, and makes the fibres of the wing 'concertina' down evenly one on top of the other. If the wing sits correctly first time throw further turns of tight thread to secure it. If it doesn't, simply remove it and try again.

Step 7

To complete, trim off the excess feather and build a neat head.

Step 8

The Blue Dun.

Paired Split Wings

The other half, so to speak, of the paired wet-fly wing is the paired dry-fly wing. The procedure for tying both is pretty much the same except for exact position and elevation, so for choice and preparation of materials please refer to the previous sequence. This type of wing may be tied in either the single or double split form, the only difference being that in the double version, two pairs of feather slips are used rather than one, giving a four-winged effect. As the technique is a very traditional one I have used an equally traditional dry fly for the tying sequence, the Greenwell's Glory.

Step 1

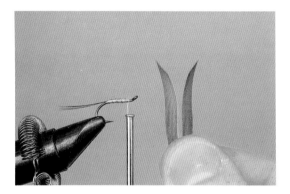

After preparing the body of the Greenwell's, select two slips of duck primary as described above (when tying very small split wings the finer fibres of starling primary give a better effect). Judge them for width. Hold them together dull sides out so that the natural curves of the feather take the tips away from each other.

Step 2

Making sure that the tips are even, place the two slips together, back to back. The prepared wing should have the same V outline as that in the illustration. Before moving on, consider the position of the tying thread. It should be set slightly farther back from the eye than for the wet-fly wing, to provide space for the hackle.

Step 3

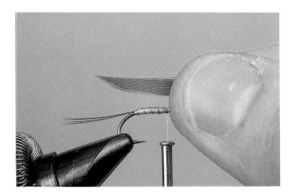

Position the prepared wing over the hook shank so that it is slightly longer than the body.

Step 4

Switching hands, hold the wing in position and throw a winging loop over the butts.

Step 5

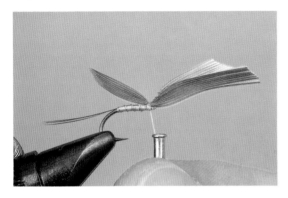

With the wing in place, secure it with further turns of thread.

Step 6

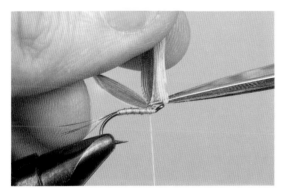

Trim off the waste feather.

Step 7

To raise the wing to the upright position, take two turns of thread behind and beneath the wing.

Step 8

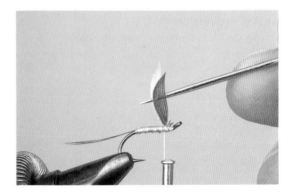

Because the webbing of duck feather is so strong, the wing slips may become joined. If this happens separate them with a dubbing needle.

Step 9

Complete the fly by adding a well-marked furnace hackle in the standard dry-fly style (*see* Chapter 7). The Greenwell's Glory.

No-Hackle Wings

A development of the standard split-winged dry fly is the No-Hackle Dun perfected by the innovative American team of Doug Swisher and Carl Richards. Otherwise known as the sidewinder wing, its tying gives the base of the fly a cupped profile, which along with widely-splayed tails is the key to the fly's floatability. Because this type of fly uses only upright wings and tails to keep it trapped in the surface film, it is inappropriate for fishing fast, turbulent streams or a heavy riffle. This matters naught, for when the fish are taking duns in calm slow glides, and proving very difficult to tempt as a result, the No-Hackle Dun comes into its own. Without the encumbrance of a hackle it produces an extremely natural profile, exactly what is required when casting to wily 'educated' fish.

Because the no-hackle wing is a style rather than a specific pattern, it can be adapted to suit individual circumstances. With variations in the colour of the body it may be used to imitate small to medium-size duns hatching off anywhere in the world.

Step 1

Because weight must be kept to a minimum a fine-wire hook is needed. Here it is a size 14 Partridge Hooper dry-fly. The tail is a V tail as described in Chapter 4; the body colour, which may be varied, is in this case a mixture of yellow and grey fur, giving an olive hue. Wind the dubbed fur only two-thirds of the way up the hook as it is at this point that the wings are added. Next select paired slips of grey duck primary, each slip being slightly wider than for the previous dressing.

Step 2

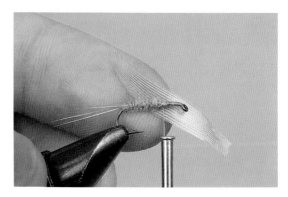

Because each wing must be tied to 'embrace' the fly's body, they should be offered up individually rather than as a pair. Each wing should therefore be positioned at the side of the hook rather than on the top. Because of the visual problem, it is easier to offer up the wing to the far side of the hook first, check its position, then add the wing on the near side.

Step 3

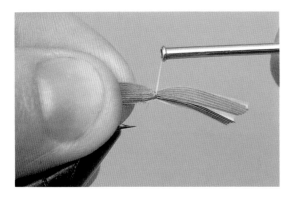

Once the wings are in position, take a single loose turn of thread over the butts then, as the second turn is made, begin to pull tight. This will prevent the wings from being pulled out of position.

Step 4

Once you are happy with the placing of the wings, bind them securely with turns of thread and remove the excess feather.

Step 5

Complete the dressing by adding a thorax of the same material as the body, finishing off with a whip finish and a coat of lacquer to the bare threads at the eye. The No-Hackle Dun.

Step 6

As a further check, the front view should be like that in the drawing, which shows the set of the wings and the angle of the tails.

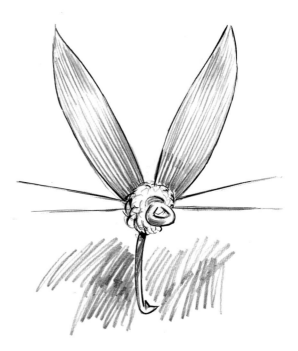

Hackle-Point Wings

Hackle points have long been used to good effect for winging mayfly spinner patterns. These imitate the dying insect trapped in the surface film and the tips of either cock or hen hackles work admirably in this situation. Originally cock hackles were more widely used, their sharp non-absorbent filaments making them ideal for a fly intended to float. Today, though, owing to vastly-improved floatants, the softer and more 'suckable' hen hackle tips have really come into their own. Indeed, many contemporary hackle-point spinners have completely dispensed with a collar hackle, leaving the floatability of the fly to the wings and tails alone. This has resulted in a much more lifelike outline.

In the illustrated tying sequence I have chosen a simple pattern with a V tail of blue dun cock hackle fibres and a body of rusty brown Superla dubbed on a size 14 Partridge barbless hook. The wings are hen hackle points of the same colour as the tail, but any of these colours or shades may be altered to imitate the insect species you have in mind. An example of this is the Caenis, in which the body should be cream, the thorax brown, and the wings and tails white. The tying sequence is exactly the same as the one illustrated. The sequence illustrates a hackleless fly, but in dressings such as Lunn's Particular and Yellow Boy the dubbed thorax is replaced by a cock hackle.

Step 1

After preparing the tail, form the body, which should end two-thirds of the way up the hook shank. It is at this point that the wing should be fixed. Select two hen hackle points of equal size. They should be as rounded as possible.

Step 2

From each hackle remove the base filaments so that the remaining tip is approximately one and a half times the length of the hook shank.

Step 3

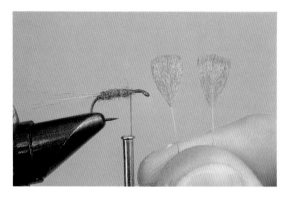

The prepared hackle points.

Step 4

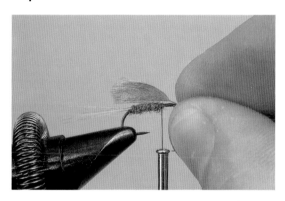

Keeping the tips even, place them together and hold the now prepared wing over the body.

Step 5

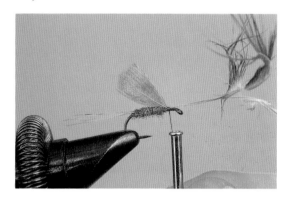

Take two or three turns of thread over the bare stalks to hold the wing in position. To give added security to the wing, fold the hackle stalks back along the body under each hackle point before trimming off the surplus. The technique is shown in step 5 of the next sequence.

Step 6

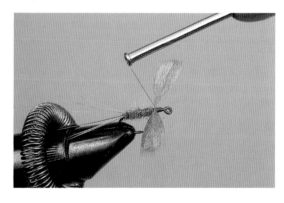

Finally, position each wing into the spent configuration with figure-of-eight turns of tying thread.

Step 7

To complete the Hackle-Point Spinner, use the same body material to dub on a thorax through the wing butts.

Fan Wings

In essence this is a beefed-up version of the previous technique, producing wings of feather tips but in this case speckled duck body plumes. Because the feathers are so large, fan wings are more applicable to the larger mayfly species of the genus Ephemera, specimens of which may be over an inch long. Various patterns in this style of tying call for a variety of duck flank types, including teal, grey mallard (either natural or dyed yellow or green) and wood duck.

Step 1

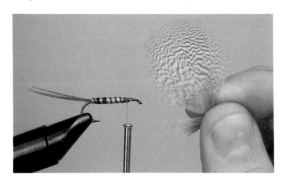

Fix a size 10 Captain Hamilton nymph hook in the vice. After tying in tails of cock pheasant tail

fibres and a body of polypropylene yarn ribbed with brown tying thread, select a matched pair of small grey mallard flank feathers.

Step 2

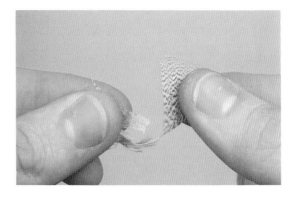

Remove the base fluff from each feather.

Step 3

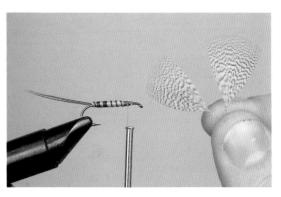

The remaining tips should be approximately one and a half times the length of the body.

Step 4

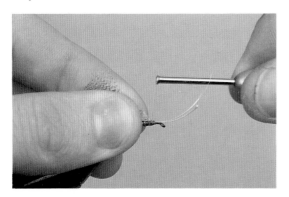

Place the flank feathers back to back, catching them in by the bare stalks with three turns of tying thread.

Step 5

Raise the feathers to the vertical by making two turns of thread behind them. Then, for added security, take the bare stalks back down the shank beneath each wing, binding down the loose ends before trimming off the waste.

Step 6

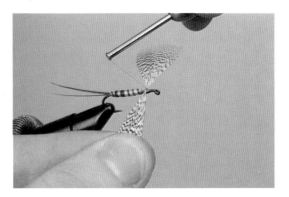

Finally, fix the wings in the horizontal spent position with figure-of-eight turns of thread.

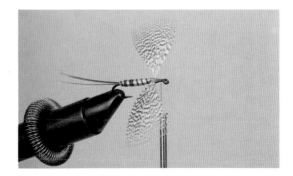

Step 7

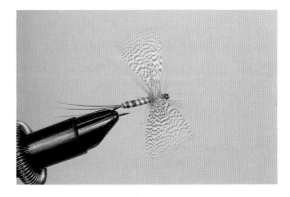

Complete the Fan-Wing Mayfly by adding a light-ginger cock hackle wound in front of and behind the wings.

Barred Teal Flank

The barred flank feathers of various duck species are used for winging many traditional wet flies. Mallard, both grey and bronze, wood duck, pintail and teal – all are used to varying degrees and all are tied in basically the same way. The latter is probably the most widely used, being the base for a whole range of dressings for both brown and rainbow trout as well as the migratory sea trout. Teal and Green, Teal and Red, Teal and Orange, Teal and Black – the list goes on. In deference to this I have used a very famous teal dressing for the following tying sequence – the Teal, Blue and Silver. This pattern, with its silver body, golden pheasant tippet tail, blue hackle and barred wing, has many of the recognition points of a small fish – probably the reason why it is so successful in catching large brown trout and sea trout, both notorious predators of fish fry.

The Teal, Blue and Silver may be dressed on a wide range of hook sizes depending on the fish and water conditions. I have used a traditional size 10 Partridge Forged Sproat G3A.

Step 1

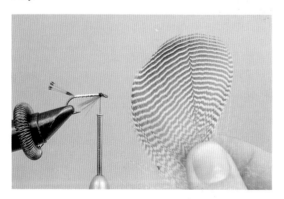

Once the body and hackle have been formed, select a well-marked teal flank feather. Preferences vary but mine is for a strongly-barred feather. Although a little more expensive, pintail flank makes a fine alternative, being more consistently marked than teal.

Step 2

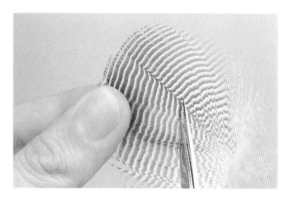

From the well-marked side of the feather stroke the tips of the fibres even and remove a slip three times the width of the intended wing.

Step 3

Fold the top third of the feather slip into its centre.

Step 4

Fold the bottom edge up so that the prepared wing now has two 'good' sides. This may then be offered up to the hook.

Step 5

Catch in the slip with the usual winging loop, then add a couple more turns to secure it in position.

Step 6

Finally, remove the excess feather at the eye, build a neat head and complete with a whip finish. The Teal, Blue and Silver.

Hackle Fibre Wings

Hackle fibres can be used to produce a sort of scaled-down version of a hair wing, and for smaller patterns, particularly for the wings of dry flies, bunches of fibres are both more convenient and easier to work. They may be split into bunches in the Wulff V style, bound spent by figure-of-eight turns of thread, or, as in the illustrated steps, tied sloping back as a 'roof' wing for a sedge fly imitation.

The Walker Red Sedge, a pattern invented by the late Richard Walker, is, like so many of his tyings, extremely simple. It is tied on a size 8, 10 or 12 ordinary down-eyed wet-fly hook, in this case a size 10 Partridge Captain Hamilton. The materials required are a few red game hackles, cock pheasant centre tail and fluorescent orange wool.

Step 1

Fix the hook in the vice and run on brown tying thread down to the bend. There catch in a short length of the wool, which is tied as a tag. This imitates the egg package of the female. The body is of chestnut pheasant tail fibres wound over a layer of wet lacquer, then left to dry. With the body complete, select a large, well-coloured red game hackle and tear off a good bunch of fibres. For larger hooks you may need to use fibres from both sides of the hackle.

Step 2

The next step is to ensure that all the tips are even. Richard Walker's original instruction was to tie in the bunch and then trim the tips square to length. I hate the clipped effect this produces, preferring to tie the wing in at the correct length in the first place. So, use a flat surface to tamp all the tips even then offer the wing up to the hook.

Step 3

Holding the wing so that the tips project a little past the bend, catch in the butts at the front of the body. Use tight turns of thread, plus a drop of lacquer to secure the smooth hackle fibres in position.

Step 4

Finish the pattern with a stiff collar hackle of red game cock and a neat, well-lacquered head. Walker's Red Sedge.

Streamer Wings

Many of the pre-marabou lure patterns included wings of one or more pairs of cock hackles. Ease of tying and superb mobility in the water have meant that marabou has all but taken over, but I still have a soft spot for this style of winging both for fry imitations and general lure dressings. Favourites such as the Black Chenille and the Black Ghost, which I have used for the tying sequence, are among many patterns which have stood the test of time and will go on catching game fish world-wide.

Step 1

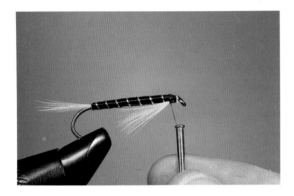

Once the tail, body and hackle of the pattern have been tied, prepare the wing.

Step 2

From a white cock cape remove two equal pairs of hackles. They should come from either side of the cape to provide opposite curves.

Step 3

Place the pairs back to back, tips even, so that the curves cancel one another out, producing a perfectly straight wing. Judge the wing for length so that it is about one and a half times that of the hook.

Step 4

Remove the fibres from the base of the hackles and catch the prepared wing in at the eye with six turns of thread.

Step 5

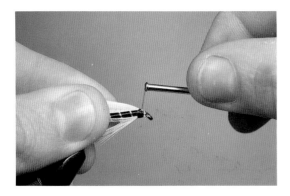

Don't remove the waste stalks right away. Instead, bend them back down the body, binding them down with further turns. This precaution will give the wing added strength.

Step 6

Now remove the stalks flush with the hackle base.

Step 7

Complete the fly by building up a neat head and adding a few coats of varnish. An optional extra is jungle cock cheeks. The Black Ghost.

The Matuka Wing

Matuka is the name of a species of New Zealand bird whose feathers were originally used for this particular method of winging. Today, though, the name has come to describe this very popular technique. Pheasant, vulturine guinea-fowl, and even fur strip are all used, along with cock hackles, and the original material has long been abandoned. Still, the substitutes – if you can call them that – are even more effective, making superb fry and bottom-grubbing patterns.

As it is a technique rather than simply a pattern, a wide range of materials can be used both for body or wing. In this case I have used a jazzed-up version of my favourite Badger Matuka, using a body of fluorescent orange chenille to make it a sure-fire killer during midsummer 'orange madness'.

Step 1

After preparing the body, which consists of a round silver rib left unwound and a length of orange chenille applied in the usual manner, select two pairs of well-marked badger hackles.

Step 2

Place the pairs together in standard streamer-wing fashion and judge for length.

Step 3

Remove the base fibres as normal, then carefully strip away the fibres along the bottom edge of the wing. Remove only those fibres which correspond with the portion of wing which will lie along the body. Doing this will help the wing sit properly.

Step 4

Again offer up the wing to judge for length. If you got it right first time, continue. If not, remove a few more fibres.

Step 5

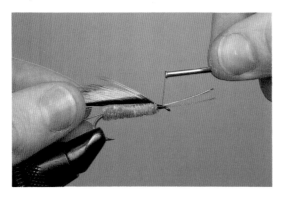

Catch the bare stalks in at the eye. Make sure that they are secure as you will need to apply tension to position the wing.

Step 6

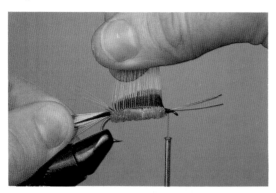

Grasping the hackle tips in the left hand, use the right to stroke the fibres to the vertical.

Step 7

Keeping tension on the wing, take hold of the silver rib and make a single tight turn at the very point where the body ends. This will secure the wing.

Step 8

Separating the fibres at intervals, wind the rib up through the hackles for five or six turns. Whatever you do, don't let go now! The spiralled rib will bind the wing tightly to the hook, forming a dorsal-fin effect. Catch in the loose end of tinsel and trim off. The drawing shows the procedure in detail.

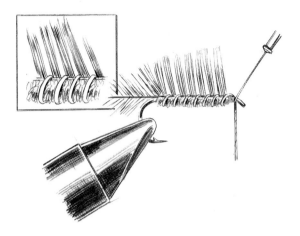

Step 9

Finish off with a collar hackle of the same hackle as the wing, and a neat, well-varnished head. The Badger Matuka.

Fur Strip

As mentioned above, fur strips may be used to wing matuka-style lures, but there is another slightly simpler way of using this wonderfully mobile yet robust material, and that is in the Zonker. The strange name shouldn't put you off what is in effect a very killing range of patterns used for all types of game fish throughout the world, both in freshwater and salt – in fact, wherever big fish eat little fish.

Although the colour of both wing and body may be altered to suit conditions and prey fish species – the Zonker is a superb bait-fish imitation – the tying method is the same for all the variations on the theme.

Step 1

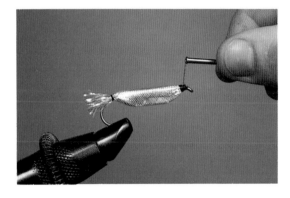

The first step in tying the Zonker range is to create the body. Though the original was of silver Mylar tubing, some of the new pearlescent types make very effective fry bodies and I have used one here. Before sliding on the Mylar, a fish-shaped underbody should be formed from rigid sticky-backed plastic strip, folded over the hook shank and trimmed to shape. Make sure, though, that the finished body doesn't intrude too far into the hook gape and diminish successful hooking. The hook I use is the tarnish-resistant JS Sea Streamer hook from Partridge in a size 4 or 6.

Step 2

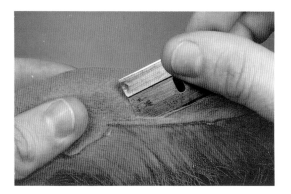

Once the body has been formed, with a razor blade cut a thin strip, approximately ³⁄₁₆ inch wide, from the skin of a rabbit. The length can be varied depending on both the size of the hook and just how long you want the wing to be. It can either end almost flush with the end of the hook shank or extend, for extra action, well beyond. The choice is yours. Cutting along the skin rather than the fur side ensures that the hair is not damaged.

Step 3

At the head catch in the fur strip after cutting it to a point. Although not shown in the photograph, it is a good idea to wet the fur strip before tying it in; this helps stretch the skin and means that the wing will not become loose during fishing. Build up a neat head and tie off the thread.

Step 4

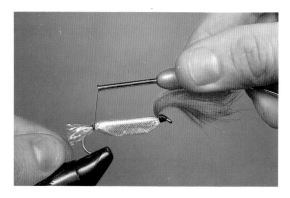

At the tail run on a length of red fluorescent floss at the point where the end of the Mylar piping was secured.

Step 5

Stretch the fur strip over the back of the shank and, judging where the turns of floss will be made, part the fur to reveal the bare skin. Make four tight turns to secure the wing to the hook.

Step 6

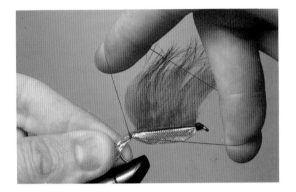

Finish off the floss-cum-tying thread with a five-turn whip finish and a coat or two of varnish.

Step 7

The pattern may be left as it is though the addition of a soft grizzle collar hackle will add that something extra. The Zonker.

Marabou

If you've read what I said about marabou tails you will realise by now that marabou is one of my favourite materials, so I make no apologies for including it again in this chapter on winging, particularly as the technique is slightly different. Marabou is great for all types of winging, especially for stillwater patterns where the lack of movement in the water itself is counteracted by the pulsating action of the feather.

The pattern I have used for the illustrated steps is a good all-round tying; it works well for high-summer rainbows and again when the water is a little coloured and a highly visible fly is needed. Hence the name – Muddy Waters.

Step 1

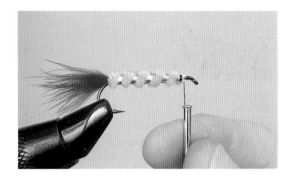

Prepare the tail, a tuft of red marabou, and the body of fluorescent yellow chenille ribbed with flat silver tinsel before proceeding. The hook is a size 6 Partridge Bucktail/Streamer, Code D4A.

Step 2

From a dyed orange marabou plume tear off a generous tuft.

Step 3

Offer the tuft up to the hook shank and judge for length. Ideally, the end of the wing should be level with that of the tail.

Step 4

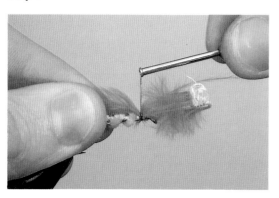

With the wing in position, take three or four tight turns over the butts. Marabou is a very compressible material, which makes tying a secure wing quite easy.

Step 5

Select another tuft of marabou, this time a slightly smaller one of yellow, and catch it in the same way as an overwing.

Step 6

With an angled cut of the scissors remove the waste butts. This angled cut will create a neat tapered effect, allowing easy winding of the hackle.

Step 7

Finish the dressing with a long mobile collar hackle of dyed red cock or hen hackle and a neat glossy black head. The Muddy Waters.

Rolled Feather Fibre

Though most types of feather fibre may be used as paired slips, it is not always possible or desirable to do so. Speckled or barred duck flank – including teal, mallard, pintail and wood duck – all work better 'rolled', particularly on smaller flies, where, owing to the fineness of the fibres towards the tips, it is difficult to obtain the correct density.

In winging terms, rolling – or, as I suppose it should be known, folding – is an ideal method for dry sedge patterns, as the wing can be formed round the body to give the 'roof' effect so obvious in the natural.

Step 1

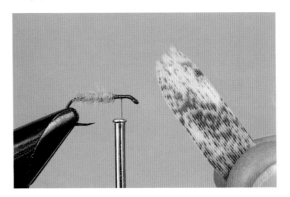

To tie a simple Roofwing Sedge, fix a fine-wire size 12 hook in the vice (in this case a Roman Moser Arrowpoint by Partridge). Run on a length of brown tying thread to the bend and dub on a body of yellow seal fur, taking it two-thirds of the way back up the hook shank. Remove a slip of feather from a speckled turkey wing quill. All the tips must be even and if they are not they should be teased into position by a gentle stroking action between finger and thumb. Because the wing is going to be folded, this slip must be three times the width of the intended wing.

Step 2

Holding the slip securely, fold the bottom edge exactly into the middle.

Step 3

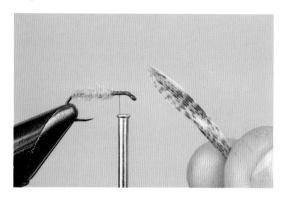

Then fold the top edge of the slip over it to produce a slip one-third the width of the original and three times as thick. This folding action produces a wing which is very strong in cross-section.

Step 4

Although once prepared a rolled wing may be tied in exactly the same way as a paired-slip wing, with a winging loop, in this case it is going to be tied more as a roof. So, instead of offering up the slip edge on to the hook, lay it on flat so that the tip projects a short way past the bend.

Step 5

The natural curve of the feather will help to shape it round the hook. When you are happy with its position secure the wing with three or four turns of thread.

Step 6

To finish, trim off the excess turkey quill and add a good-quality brown cock hackle. In larger patterns you may need more than one hackle feather to produce a nice thorax spread. The Roofwing Sedge.

Folded-Wing Cases

As a follow-on to tying a folded wing, I have included a secondary, closely-related technique – that of tying folded wing cases. Though not a true winging method, it does at least have the merit of imitating an insect's wings still locked within the nymphal skin. It is ideal, therefore, for laying over the thorax of any mayfly, stonefly or dragonfly nymphal pattern.

Most materials, so long as they are flat and able to take a fold, can be used for this method, including raffia, plastic strip and feather fibre. My preference is for the latter, for, although it is the most difficult of the three to use, it not only produces a very lifelike result but also lacks the hard 'clinical' effect of the smoother products.

Various types of feather fibre may be used. The larger the pattern being dressed, the coarser the texture of the feather can be. For small mayfly patterns duck or pheasant wing can be used, while for larger dragonfly and stonefly nymphs, goose and turkey come into their own. The only other consideration is colour. Due to the pre-dominantly dark hues of the wing cases of aquatic insect larvae before emergence, blacks and browns and greys will be found the most useful.

Reflecting this, the illustrated sequence uses dark-brown turkey tail, the pattern being an imitation of a large, dark-brown stonefly nymph.

Step 1

Fix a size 6 Partridge nymph hook in the vice and run a length of brown tying thread down to the bend. There catch in two fibres of woodchuck or peccary body hair as tails, plus 2 inches of thick brown thread. If a weighted dressing is required, weight may now be added (*see* Chapter 9). If not, the body may be completed by dubbing brown Superla two-thirds of the way back up the shank. That done, take a strip of dark-brown turkey tail three times the width of the intended wing cases and fold it in the same way as for the previous technique. Catch the prepared strip in by the tips at the point where the dubbed body ends.

Step 2

Dub on another pinch of brown Superla, winding it on so it covers half of the remaining bare shank. Take hold of the turkey tail by the butts and bring it over towards the eye. But, instead of pulling it taut, insert a medium-size darning needle into the loop. Gently ease the needle back down the shank so that the loose turkey tail folds back on itself for approximately 1/8 inch. Catch in the butts with three turns of thread. As the needle is removed from the loop, work the folded turkey down on to the top of the shank with your thumb and forefinger until a definite fold is produced. It is important to use the very tips of the tail, which, being softer and better webbed, are easier to fold without splitting than the butts.

Step 3

Some patterns require only one set of wing cases but this one calls for two, so the procedure should now be repeated to produce double wing cases. Before folding back the turkey strip for the second time, wind on a hackle of grouse or a substitute and divide it into two bunches. To complete the pattern, two fibres of turkey tail may be left to form antennae, after which a neat head and a solid whip finish should be made.

Polypropylene

Apart from the previously-mentioned natural materials such as duck quill, hackle points and hair, there are other – man-made – products which are finding increasing use in dry-fly winging. Perhaps the best known is polypropylene. Its fibres are very light and make superb easy-to-tie wings, especially on no-hackle spent patterns. For many years anglers in Britain were quite content to use dressings to imitate spinners which were merely light-hackled standard winged dries. These were usually a compromise which never fished correctly in the surface film as the natural insect would. Recently we have seen more anglers taking a lead from the United States and fishing no-hackle spinners. In clear glides and on stillwaters these prove much more effective than normal patterns, particularly when trying to tempt wily late-season fish which have made it through the summer.

The beauty of the Poly-Winged Spinner is that it sits with wings outstretched, trapped in the surface tension just like the natural. Although the colours of the body and the size of the hook can be altered to match the naturals encountered, the tying sequence is the same for all. The illustrated sequence begins with the tails and the body already dressed, ready for the wing to be tied in.

Step 1

After dressing a tail and a body on a suitable hook, anything from a fine-wire size 12 to a 20 or even smaller, you are ready to tie in the wing. Leave approximately one-quarter of the shank free from dressing to accept this. Take an inch-long piece of polypropylene yarn and offer it up to the hook. Suitable colours vary from white to pale grey. Intended to imitate the diaphanous wings of the spinner, it should be as translucent as possible.

Step 2

Place the yarn on the hook and catch it in half-way along with a simple turn of thread.

Step 3

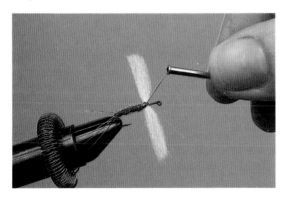

With figure-of-eight turns of thread bind in the wing securely so that approximately ½ inch projects from each side of the hook.

Step 4

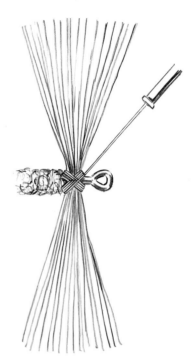

In close-up you can see the route the thread takes to ensure that the wings are bound in securely and sit at 90 degrees to the hook shank.

Step 5

Dub a small amount of the body material on to waxed thread and wind it in behind, through and in front of the wings to form a thorax. Finish off the dressing at this point.

Step 6

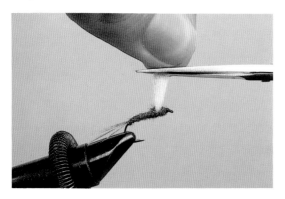

The final step is to trim the wings to length. Take the ends between finger and thumb, pulling them above the hook shank. This ensures that both wings will be of identical size. Then, with scissors, cut them so that each wing is approximately the same length as the hook shank. With a dubbing needle spread the fibres of the wings to give them maximum area. This will help the fly to float.

Step 7

The front view shows the angle of the finished wing, tied spent.

Step 8

The completed Poly-Winged Spinner.

The Married Feather Wing

As an end to this chapter on winging it would be remiss not to include the pinnacle of the fly dresser's craft – the fully-dressed salmon fly. Though today most fly-caught salmon fall to simple concoctions of hair and hackle, towards the latter half of the nineteenth and in the first half of the twentieth century the vogue was for wonderful, intricate dressings containing materials from many exotic locations. Toucan, blue chatterer, florican bustard, Indian crow – all were used to create patterns the like of which most of us can only dream about.

Even though these materials and many others are now unobtainable – as a result, thankfully, of conservation measures rather than extinction – there is still plenty of scope for tyers who wish to explore this most aesthetic challenge. At worst, unobtainable materials can simply be omitted, but substitutes are available for many of them so we still have the opportunity to produce some framable flies for the rod room or the study.

Many of the fully-dressed patterns may appear very difficult to tie, but most of the steps are exactly the same as those described for much simpler patterns. There are just more of them. Perhaps the trickiest process is the marrying or 'building' of a wing from various strips of coloured feather fibre. As it is integral to a high proportion of salmon patterns, and the occasional trout wet fly such as the Parmachene Belle, it is included here.

The pattern I have used as the example is the Silver Doctor, a tying with a long tradition. It also has the advantage of using materials most of which are still obtainable. Traditionally a tapered-shank hook and a gut eye were used, but to give this fly a contemporary feel I have used the Partridge Bartleet salmon iron, a hook with a loop eye and a lovely traditional shape to the bend and barb.

Step 1

After fixing the hook in the vice, run on a length of black tying thread from the eye to slightly round the bend in neat touching turns. There tie in a tag of round silver tinsel backed up with golden yellow floss. The tail is of golden pheasant crest topped with blue kingfisher, a substitute for blue chatterer, whilst the butt is of scarlet wool, dubbed on. The body is flat silver tinsel ribbed with fine oval silver. The hackle is a pale-blue hackle overlaid with widgeon or light teal flank at the throat. The underwing is a few strands of golden pheasant tippet, overlaid with strips of golden pheasant centre tail.

Step 2

As the wing is to be made up of strips of coloured feather fibre, take goose feathers dyed red, blue and yellow and from each remove paired slips in much the same way as for the paired wet-fly wing.

Step 3

The difference is that here the slips should be much finer, containing only two or three fibres each.

Step 4

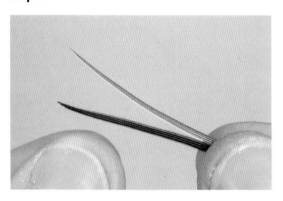

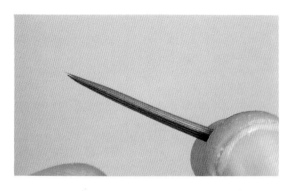

The strips may then be married together. This is done by aligning the strips from the same side of each feather together, points even.

Step 5

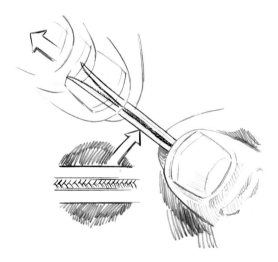

Then between forefinger and thumb gently stroke the strips together. The barbs on each fibre, which are so well pronounced in wildfowl, will help the strips to join in much the same way as a zip-fastener works.

Step 6

Don't try to join all the strips together at once but add each strip one at a time, slowly building up the wing. The order from the bottom should be yellow, blue, then red.

Step 7

That done, further thin strips or light mottled turkey tail, peacock wing and bustard or a substitute should be added to produce two paired wings of equal size.

Step 8

Place each wing either side of the underwing and, after making sure that the tips are even, catch in with a winging loop. Because you are working with so much feather you may need to manipulate the married slips into position, easing them down with forefinger and thumb as the thread is tightened. If the slips should twist or split, simply remove them, repair and try again.

Step 9

To complete the fly, remove the excess feather at the eye, then add an overwing of bronze mallard strips, plus narrow strips of teal and barred summer duck laid down each side. Finally, golden pheasant crests should be laid over all and the head finished off with scarlet wool dubbed on prior to the whip finish. The Silver Doctor.

Contrast the gaudy hues of kingfisher and dyed goose herl with the delicate mottling of hen pheasant.

9 The Weighting Game

The action and presentation of a fly depends much on its style of tying. Dry flies float, wet flies sink, and emergers sit precariously in the surface film. Each has its place, possessing properties which allow the angler to fish it under specific circumstances. It's all very logical. For example, a good hatch of blue-winged olives is in progress and the trout are consistently popping off the duns as they float downstream. Obviously a suitable dry imitation is going to be the most effective ploy. Likewise, when chironomids are being taken in that curious half-way house when the adult is trapped at the very point of emergence, a pattern which mimics the phenomenon and fishes right in the surface film is the best choice.

This is all well and good, but when it comes to the wet fly the rules alter slightly. Yes, of course the fly should sink, but at what rate, and, more important, to what depth? Once we leave the realms of the visual it becomes much more difficult to decide just how our flies should be fished. Temperature and water depth figure highly in the choice. Cold early-season conditions often mean the fish lying hard on the bottom feeding on insect nymphs and larvae as well as crustaceans, including shrimp and water hoglouse.

But even if we have a good idea just where the fish are we still have to get the fly to the correct depth. We can, of course, use sinking lines, but it is very difficult to present a nymph in the 'dead drift' style with a sinker; harder still to perceive those gentle pauses of the line that so often mean a fish. The best idea is to use a floating line with a long leader, weighting the fly itself to make it sink.

There are various ways of adding weight, each depending on the way the fly is going to be fished. In most patterns, notably imitative and suggestive ones, the weight is added as an underbody before dressing and ranges from turns of copper wire, just to help small nymph patterns break cleanly through the surface film, to consecutive layers of lead strip, designed for fishing big nymph and streamer patterns in very deep or turbulent water.

But weighting a fly not only makes it sink quicker; it also changes the action of the fly. This phenomenon can work both for and against the angler. For instance, dressings which need to appear light and ethereal, such as salmon flies, are best fished deep on a sinking line, which allows the fly to flutter seductively in the current. Here the action of the fly remains the same; only the depth at which it is fished alters. Conversely, patterns such as lead-head jigs and Dog Nobblers, with their light tails and heavily-weighted heads, not only fish deep but do so in a ducking, diving action, which proves so killing. Obviously, here the inherent weight of the fly is what makes it so effective: fishing a long-tailed unweighted streamer on a sinking line isn't nearly so productive.

So weighting a fly can fulfil a variety of purposes and it is up to the tyer to decide which fits the fly and the circumstances in which it is fished.

Wound Lead Wire

The simplest method of weighting a fly is the mere addition of a few turns of lead wire. This particular style works well for all types of pattern requiring extra weight, from streamers and hair wings to large bottom-grubbing nymphs.

Step 1

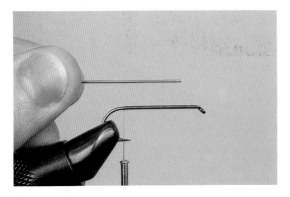

After fixing the required hook securely in the vice, run a length of tying thread down to the bend in tight, touching turns. Take 2 inches of lead wire. In the illustrations the hook used is a size 8 Partridge/Bucktail Streamer and the thickness of the lead wire is commensurate with this. For smaller hooks reduce the thickness of the lead wire accordingly.

Step 2

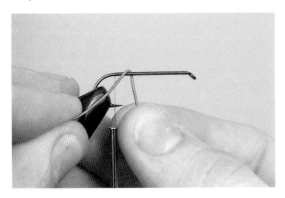

Holding both ends of the lead wire, loop it over the hook shank.

Step 3

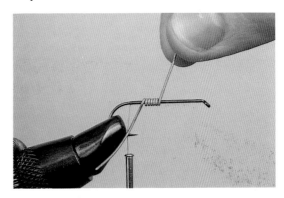

Starting a quarter of the way up the hook shank, begin winding the wire.

Step 4

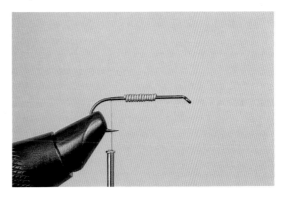

Keep winding the lead wire up towards the eye in neat touching turns until half the hook has been covered. Remove the excess wire by simply pulling it off with the fingers. Lead wire is soft enough to allow this.

Step 5

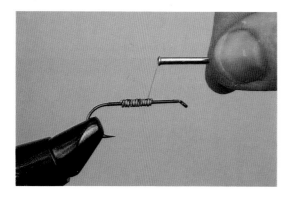

To keep the lead underbody in position take turns of thread up over it, finishing off at the eye. As a further precaution add a coat of varnish.

Parallel Lead Wire

Lead wire doesn't have to be wound; it can also be added in short lengths attached to the sides of the hook shank. This method increases the effective width of the hook shank, making it ideal for tying flat-bodied patterns, including dragonfly and stonefly nymph imitations.

Step 1

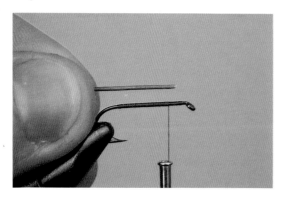

After fixing the hook in the vice run on a length of tying thread to the bend. Select the appropriate width of lead wire.

Step 2

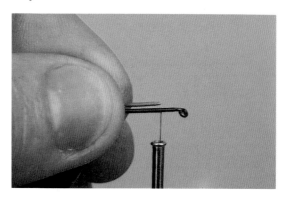

Cut the wire into short lengths, approximately half to two-thirds the length of the hook shank. Make sure that the ends are cut in a taper rather than square.

Step 3

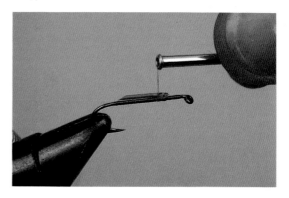

Offer one length up to the hook, binding it securely to the side of the shank with neat touching turns. Wind down to the bend before working back up the shank, securing a second length of lead wire to the other side.

Step 4

Complete by covering the underbody with tight turns of thread, making sure that the wire lengths run along the sides of the hook and don't pull either above or beneath. To further secure the wire in place run on a few drops of varnish or cyanoacrylate adhesive.

Lead Strip

A slightly more complicated method of weighting a fly comes in the form of the tapered lead strip. A number of strips of lead foil of varying widths are bound on the top of a hook shank to give a shaped and heavy underbody. This method is particularly applicable to large nymph and shrimp imitations. Because all the lead is on the top of the shank, the hook fishes point up, which reduces the risk of hooking up on bottom weed or other obstructions. Also, because of the extra weight, it is ideal for the big, very quick-sinking nymphs used for stalking large clearwater trout.

The required thin lead foil strip can be obtained either from a laboratory supplier or, more cheaply, from round the neck of a wine bottle.

Step 1

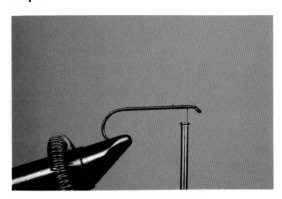

Fix the hook – in this instance a size 8 Partridge Streamer/Bucktail pattern – in the vice and run a length of tying thread down to the bend in tight butted turns. Take the thread back up the shank towards the eye in a more open spiral. This unevenness gives a key which helps the underbody to grip.

Step 2

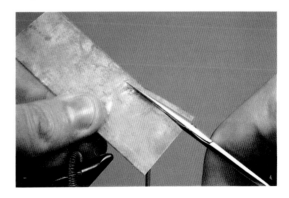

Cut a very thin strip of lead foil, no more than twice the width of the hook shank.

Step 3

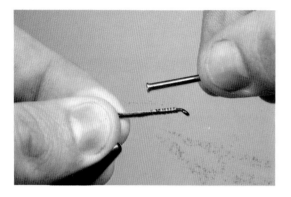

Catch the strip in at the eye and bind it down the total length of the hook shank. Remove the excess.

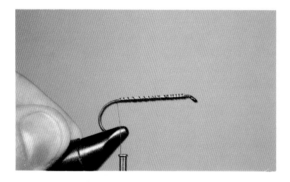

Step 4

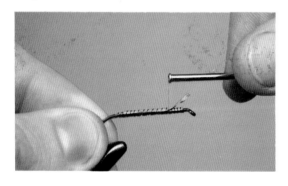

Catch in the excess strip again a little further up the shank from where the previous strip ended. Bind it down securely, finishing a short distance from the eye.

Step 5

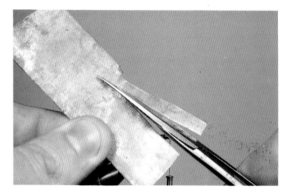

Cut a second strip, a little wider this time.

Step 6

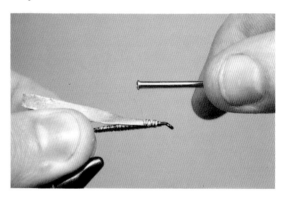

Catch it in just short of the eye and bind it down on top of the previous strips. Repeat the process until the desired weight is reached. The number of strips required will depend on the size of the hook.

Step 7

The completed lead underbody.

Copper Wire

Copper wire is far less dense than lead and so is unsuitable for patterns fished very deep off a floating line. Where copper wire does score is in very tiny dressings, where the fine wire doesn't produce excessive bulk, and for larger patterns intended to fish a foot or so below the surface. Here, particularly in the case of ephemerid nymphs, turns of wire can be added to give bulk to the thorax, simulating the profile of the natural.

Step 1

Holding both ends of a length of copper wire taut, loop it over the shank and begin to wind the right end over the left, catching it in a short distance from the eye. It is similar to the technique used for catching in tying thread.

Step 2

Secure the waste end with several turns of wire and break it off.

Step 3

Wind the wire in close turns to a point opposite the hook point.

Step 4

Wind the wire back up the shank and continue winding back and forth, over a shorter distance each time, until an oval thorax shape is produced.

Step 5

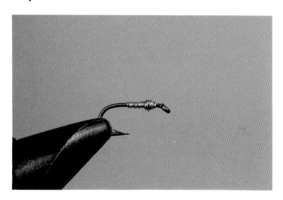

Finally a sharp tug breaks the wire. The addition of a coat of varnish before dressing the fly will improve durability.

Lead Shot

Lead shot as a means of weighting flies is nothing new. It has become increasingly popular, though, as a result of the massive attention paid to the Dog Nobbler and its successors, in which a heavily-weighted head combined with a long, sinuous tail of marabou produced a breed of lure which took the British stillwater trout scene by storm. In Britain lead shot is now banned as a result of conservation measures introduced to reduce swan deaths attributed to lead poisoning. However, substitutes are now available which, though slightly larger for the same weight, still allow lead-heads and Dog Nobbler-style lures to be tied.

Step 1

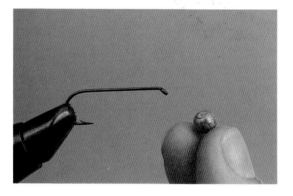

After fixing a size 8 or 10 Partridge Bucktail/ Streamer hook in the vice, select an AAA or BB size split lead shot.

Step 2

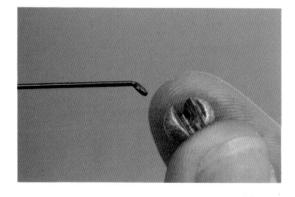

Open the split up to its full extent. Often the shot will be partially closed as a result of being jostled around in the packet.

Step 3

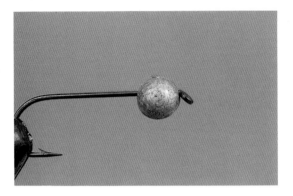

Place the shot over the hook shank so that it lies flush with the eye, and squeeze it in place with simple finger pressure.

Step 4

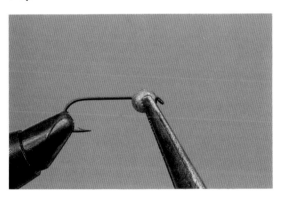

Allow a few drops of cyanoacrylate adhesive to run into the split before pinching the shot firmly closed with a pair of pliers. Firm pressure is very important as this form of adhesive bonds with strong contact.

Step 5

To complete the process, the shot may be coated with black varnish or silver paint. As a further refinement a pair of eyes may be added (*see* Chapter 10).

Lead Eyes

Taking the properties of the lead-head lure one step further, the obvious progression is to produce a range of weights specifically for tying flies. These are now being marketed under the name of Lead-eyes and are dumb-bell shaped for balance and ease of tying and to produce lifelike eyes for various weighted nymph and fry imitations. Because of the wide range of sizes, weight can be varied according to the conditions under which the fly must fish. Some are heavy enough to use for sand bumping when fishing in the salt whilst others are light enough even for small damsel and dragonfly nymphs. Either way, the Lead-eyes may be attached above or beneath the hook shank. Above the shank means that the hook fishes point up, preventing weed fouling and dulled points; beneath, and the fly will fish as normal.

Step 1

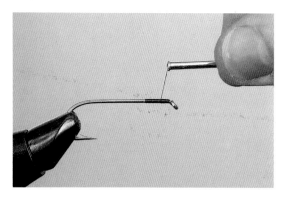

Fix a size 6 Partridge JS Sea Streamer hook in the vice and run a length of tying thread from the eye a third of the way down the hook shank. This will provide a firm base for the dumb-bell.

Step 2

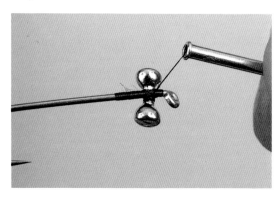

Holding the dumb-bell – in this case on the underside of the hook shank – take two or three turns of tying thread over the join to catch it in position.

Step 3

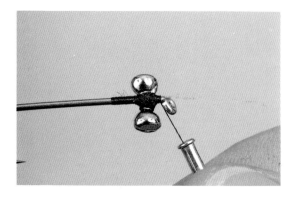

Continue to make figure-of-eight turns round the shank and join until the dumb-bell is secured firmly in place.

Step 4

To make the eyes very robust, allow a few drops of cyanoacrylate adhesive to soak into the bindings.

Step 5

As with the lead shot, Lead-eyes may be given a coat of black varnish or have eyes painted on.

Bead Chain Eyes

This method of weighting a fly is similar to the last. The main advantage is that it is cheaper and because the eyes are of hollow metal beads they aren't as dense as the lead eyes. This allows the same bulbous eye effect to be produced but with less weight and, consequently, easier casting. Even so, there is still enough weight to produce the 'kick' in long-tailed marabou lures.

Step 1

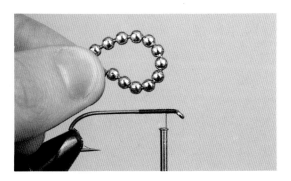

After fixing the hook – in this case a size 8 JS Sea Streamer – in the vice, run on a length of black tying thread a short way behind the eye. Select a length of bead chain.

Step 2

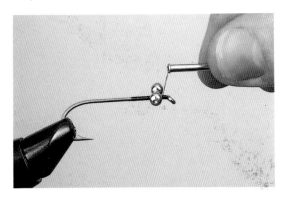

With a pair of pliers or metal cutters, snip off a pair of beads. Hold the pair in position with two turns of thread.

Step 3

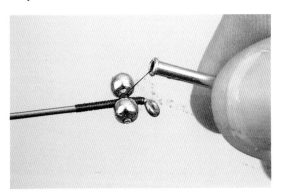

As the beads are not so heavy for their size as lead eyes, they can be attached to the upper side of the hook shank without causing the hook to fish upside down. As with the lead eyes, though, keep making figure-of-eight turns of thread until the beads are held securely.

Step 4

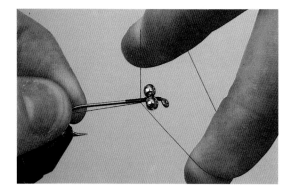

Make a whip finish and remove the excess thread.

Step 5

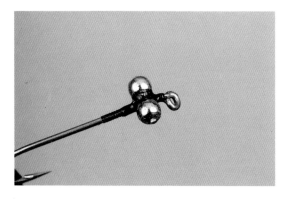

Add a few drops of cyanoacrylate adhesive to the threads and leave to dry. The beads may then be painted with various coloured lacquers to produce eyes or left their original shiny silver.

Buoyant Eyes

To end this chapter on weighting, it is a good idea to consider its opposite – buoyancy. Apart from the technique of tying in strips of expanded plastic foam under body dressings, or as a shell back as in the Buoyant Baby Doll, small polystyrene balls can be used to ensure that emergent nymph dressings float right in the surface film.

The latter method is an integral part of the Booby series, a range of buoyant-headed flies designed by Gordon Fraser. These tyings come in a wide range of colours and forms and can be fished either on a floating line or on a sinking line with short leader, which gives a dipping and rising action that has fooled some very big trout.

Step 1

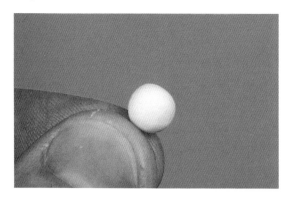

This is the standard polystyrene ball. It may be used either singly in emergent nymphs, such as John Goddard's Suspender Buzzer, or as a pair for the Booby series.

Step 2

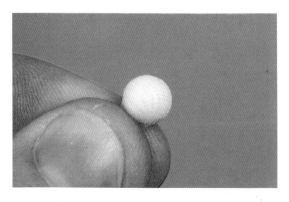

In order to tie the polystyrene ball to the hook it must be enclosed within a piece of white nylon stocking. To do this simply place the stocking over the ball and stretch it tight.

Step 3

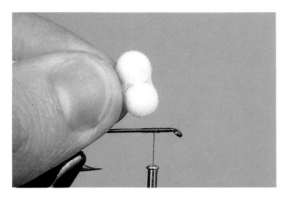

To tie the Booby, fix a size 10 Captain Hamilton nymph hook in the vice and run a length of brown tying thread on at the eye, taking it a short way down the shank and then back up again in neat touching turns. This will provide a stable base for the eyes. That accomplished, place two polystyrene balls of equal size inside a piece of stocking.

Step 4

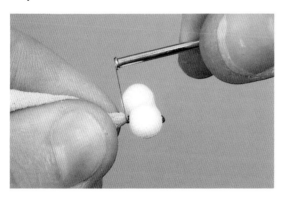

Place the eyes on the top side of the shank so that the open end of the stocking lies back towards the bend. Catch it in with three turns of thread.

Step 5

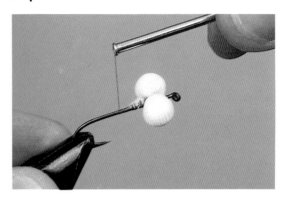

Once they are in place, make figure-of-eight turns round and through the eyes. This will cause the stocking to stretch even more, holding the balls securely. With a sharp pair of scissors remove the excess stocking.

Step 6

To complete the dressing, which in this case is for the Yellow Marabou-tailed Booby, carry the thread on down to the bend and there catch in a tuft of yellow marabou, plus a couple of inches of oval gold tinsel. Dub on yellow seal fur as a body and wind the rib up to the eyes before adding a thorax of hare fur and a solid whip finish. The Booby.

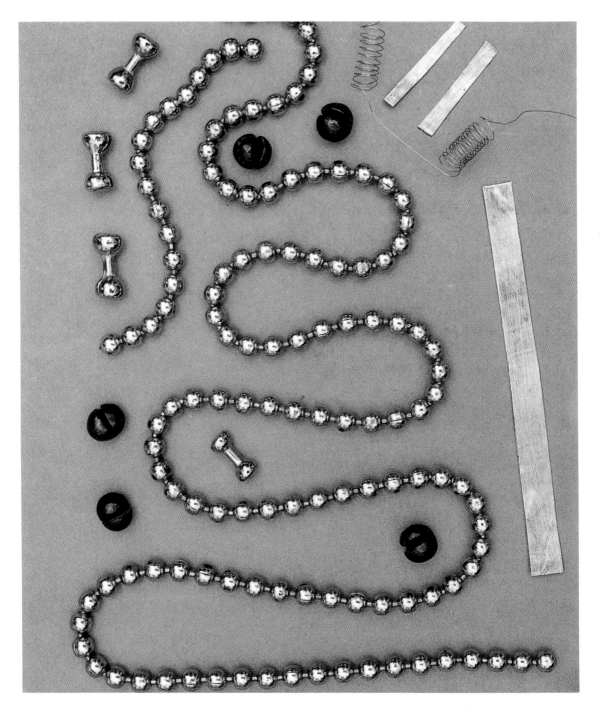

Metal beads, lead eyes, wires, strips and shot all play their part in the
weighting game.

10　The Finishing Touch

Although the primary intention in tying a fly is to catch a fish on it, to some tyers the satisfaction derived from tying a 'perfect' example of the pattern is an end in itself. To others it is merely a practical matter and a fly is built simply to catch fish, with little care paid to refinements. The argument is always that 'The fish don't mind, do they?' Well, there is a middle ground, where the tyer can not only produce fish-catching flies but neat, well-finished ones too. In many ways it is always better to tie a tidy, properly-finished fly. Not only does it give you a spur to go on to more difficult and testing patterns, but a neat fly is invariably more strongly tied, better able to stand up to the rigours of casting and the impact of a hard take. So, even though a scruffy fly may seem quicker to tie, taking a little more time ensures that your flies will keep their dressings and their fish-catching ability together for as long as possible.

Heads

Giving your flies an extra touch to set them apart is not difficult. Perhaps the simplest method concentrates on the head, making sure that it is nicely shaped and well lacquered. This is extremely important for larger wet flies and streamers, where the head can really set the dressing off. What is more is that a smooth lacquer-soaked head protects the tying thread wraps at the eye, preventing the whip finish from coming apart. For most purposes a simple cellulose varnish or lacquer as generally sold for fly heads is quite sufficient. Veniard's Cellire is a good example, and is available in a wide range of colours as well as clear. For most heads I prefer the latter, using the colour of the tying thread to shine through.

Whichever type, though, I always find that it is a good idea to use more than one coat, applied in small drops with the tip of a dubbing needle. If the consistency of the lacquer is kept just right (thinners should be added as the lacquer thickens in the bottle), the first coat will soak right into the thread wraps, giving extra adhesion to wing, thread and hackle alike. Further coats may be added, with each allowed to dry before the next is applied, until a shiny teardrop effect is produced.

The only minor drawback of the cellulose-based lacquers is that with time they will dry fully and eventually crack. On small flies with a rapid turnover this matters little, but on more elaborate streamers and salmon flies it can be a real drawback. Because of this, for larger patterns I prefer a vinyl-based product such as Vycoat. The advantage of vinyl is that it never dries fully, remaining very tough and resistant but never shrinking enough to crack. Unfortunately, vinyl too has a drawback in that it turns white when soaked in water, which ruins the effect of coloured heads. This problem can be solved by using clear vinyl in combination with a coloured cellulose. For instance, for a black streamer head, the first coat would be of clear vinyl allowed to soak well into the thread, the second would be black cellulose, and the third, added before the second is fully dry, would be of clear vinyl again. Because the coat of black cellulose isn't dry it actually permeates the vinyl and prevents it changing colour in the water. The final effect is wonderfully smooth, shiny and lasting.

Eyes

On some dressings, particularly fry imitations, the addition of a pair of eyes can do a great deal to improve the overall look and effectiveness of the tying. Eyes may be applied to a whole host of lures and streamers, either to lead eyes or shot, or straight on to the sides of a normally lacquered head. Whichever way, the technique of application is basically the same. Again, coloured cellulose lacquer may be used, or even model maker's paint, which comes in a wide range of colours, including fluorescents, which can produce some very interesting effects.

The best method of producing eyes is to use a dubbing or large sewing needle. Unlike regular varnishing, though, instead of using small drops and working them over the thread, a larger drop should be lifted on the point of the needle. That done, merely touch the side of the head with the side of the droplet. The lacquer will be transferred to the head, producing a circle or oval of colour. If you are unsure of the technique practise it by making circles on a piece of plastic until you are able to control the size and shape of the droplet.

The normal course is to produce an eye with a light base, such as white or yellow, with a darker pupil, usually of black. Of course, any combination may be used, including three colours – which looks very effective and mimics the tri-coloured eyes of many small fish fry. Each consecutive circle must be slightly smaller than the previous one, hence the necessity to control the size of the drop and to be able to do this consistently so that both eyes are identical.

The fly in the sequence below is a palmered yellow Dog Nobbler.

Step 1

Once the dressing is complete you are ready to add the eyes if required. Here the split shot giving weight to the head has already been given a coat of black paint.

Step 2

Choose the base colour. With a black-painted head a contrasting colour should be used. In this case it is yellow, but it could quite easily be white. Using the point of a dubbing needle, pick up a good-size drop of lacquer and simply place it against the fly's head. If the head is slightly lower than the needle point, gravity will transfer the lacquer, which will spread into a thin circle. Use one steady movement to create the circle of colour rather than dabbing around the edges.

Step 3

The technique produces a nice even result. Repeat on the other side of the head, as with the subsequent steps.

Step 4

Allow the lacquer to dry slightly before adding a second drop. You can, at this stage, simply put in a pupil of black, or, as here, another colour. Make sure that the circle is a little smaller than the first.

Step 5

Once the second colour has dried a little, add the final part of this three-stage eye, a black pupil. The lacquer eye.

Other types of eyes, such as the Frog or Optic eyes, which have plastic whites with movable pupils, may also be used. These are simply bound on or glued to the sides of the head with an epoxy resin. In this case epoxy works better than the cyanoacrylate 'super' glues as it allows the eyes to be stuck even to the sides of Muddler heads. If you want to be really flash you can even obtain the glass eyes used by taxidermists. These are obviously of superb quality, though expensive, and look fantastic on large saltwater Muddlers. If you want to take your bait-fish imitations to the peak, then this is the way to go!

Further Reading

Since this book is intended as a guide to fly-tying techniques rather than patterns, the books listed below are recommended as a source of many of the dressings in use today, as well as some of the more traditional tyings.

Church, Bob, *Bob Church's Guide to Trout Flies* (The Crowood Press, 1987)
Courtney Williams, A., *A Dictionary of Trout Flies* (A. & C. Black, 1973)
Goddard, John, *Trout Fly Recognition* (A. & C. Black, 1966)
Harris, J. R., *An Angler's Entomology* (Collins, 1952)
Jorgensen, Poul, *Poul Jorgensen's Modern Trout Flies* (Ernest Benn, 1979)
Pryce-Tannatt, T. E., *How to Dress Salmon Flies* (A. & C. Black, 1986)
Roberts, John, *The New Illustrated Dictionary of Trout Flies* (Allen & Unwin, 1986)
Robson, Kenneth, *Robson's Guide* (Beekay, 1985)
Taverner, Eric, *Fly Tying for Salmon* (Seeley Service, 1942)

Index